Barclay Rubincam

A Retrospective

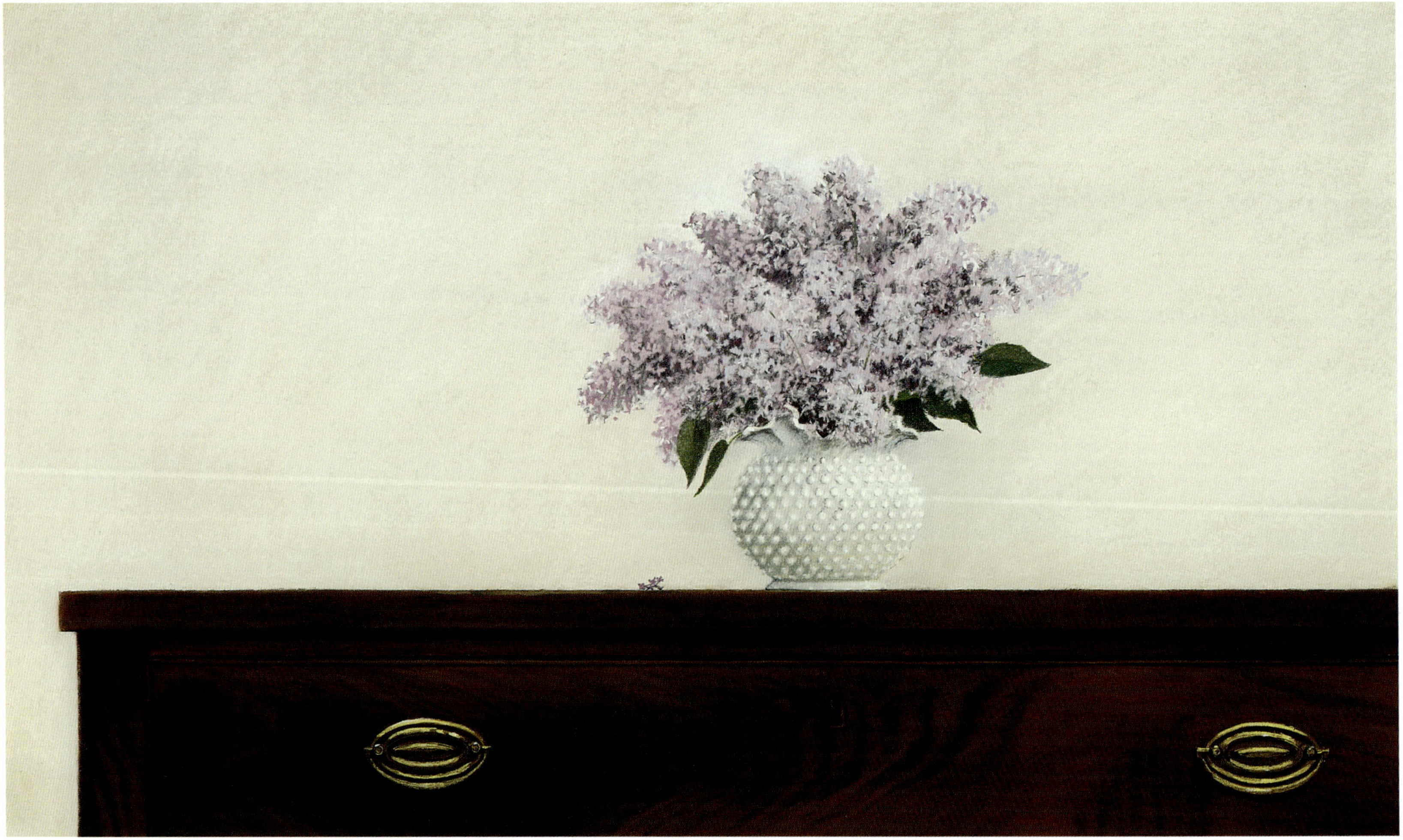

63. Lilacs on a Chest

Barclay Rubincam
A Retrospective

Exhibition Essay by
Beverly B. Sheppard

Catalogue by
Daphne S. Landis
Beverly B. Sheppard
Roland H. Woodward

Chester County Historical Society
West Chester, Pennsylvania

1998

Credits

***Barclay Rubincam: A Retrospective* is sponsored by Suburban Cable.**

Cover illustration: **Pewter Country, Cat. 51,** *Collection of Gerry Lenfest*
Frontispiece: **Lilacs on a Chest, Cat. 63,** *Collection of Edward and Jean E. Cotter*
Essay photographs courtesy of Mrs. Barclay Rubincam (Figs. 1, 6, 7, 8, 9, 11, 12, 13) and Barbara Rubincam (Figs. 2, 3, 4, 5, 10)

This catalogue accompanies an exhibition held from September 25, 1998 through April 4, 1999 at Chester County Historical Society, West Chester, Pennsylvania. The exhibition and catalogue are sponsored by Suburban Cable. Additional support provided by the Institute of Museum and Library Services (a federal agency) and the Commonwealth of Pennsylvania.

Library of Congress Cataloging-in-Publication Data
Sheppard, Beverly, 1941–
Barclay Rubincam: a retrospective/exhibition essay by Beverly B. Sheppard: catalogue by Daphne S. Landis, Beverly B. Sheppard, Roland H. Woodward: edited by Roland H. Woodward.
p. cm.
Catalog of an exhibition held at the Chester County Historical Society, Sept. 25, 1998–Apr. 4, 1999.
ISBN 0-929706-09-9
1. Rubincam, Barclay. 1920–1978—Exhibitions. I. Rubincam, Barclay, 1920–1978. II. Landis, Daphne S. III. Woodward, Roland H., 1947– . IV. Chester County Historical Society (West Chester, Pa.) V. Title.
ND237.R728A4 1998
759.13—dc21 98–41621
CIP

Edited by Roland H. Woodward
Catalogue photography by George J. Fistrovich
Designed by Suzanne DeMott Gaadt, West Chester, Pennsylvania
Printed and bound by Piccari Press, Inc., Warminster, Pennsylvania

Foreword and Acknowledgements

Barclay Rubincam's work fuses history and art. He offers the viewer an appreciation and reverence for the past that transforms his work into a series of scenes in which significant events are played out, that give us the opportunity to reflect on the Chester County landscape, or that cause us to find connections between the art we see and our own thoughts about the history of this region.

Chester County Historical Society is very pleased to present this retrospective of Barclay Rubincam's art. Twenty years have passed since the artist's death and we are poised for the celebration of West Chester's bicentennial. Fifty years ago, in 1949, an illustrated historical map of West Chester by Rubincam was part of West Chester's sesquicentennial celebration. What an appropriate time to offer the public an opportunity to discover, revisit, and appreciate the work of this much admired Chester County artist.

This exhibition and catalogue have been over a year in planning and development. Many people have made important contributions, and we wish to acknowledge and thank them for their efforts.

- To all of our lenders, who agreed to share their paintings with the public and who so graciously made them available for photography and research.
- To Daphne S. Landis, who served as our guest curator, and who shared her extensive knowledge about Rubincam's work. Daphne also organized the Chester County Art Association's one-week Rubincam exhibit in 1990.
- To Beverly B. Sheppard, formerly associate director of Chester County Historical Society and now deputy director of the Institute of Museum and Library Services, for her insightful catalogue essay, and for her critical role in preparing the exhibition and catalogue.
- To Caroline H. Rubincam, Barclay's widow, who is an enthusiastic champion of her husband's work. Caroline generously shared her knowledge, art works, photographs, and reminiscences, which helped shape the exhibition and gave all of us working on it a sense of really coming to know Barclay Rubincam.
- To Barbara Rubincam, Barclay's sister, who shared photographs and wonderful stories of her older brother.
- To George J. Fistrovich, photographer and Suzanne DeMott Gaadt, designer, for their skill and expertise in preparing this catalogue.
- To the staff of Chester County Historical Society, who have ably and patiently worked on the exhibit and catalogue with their usual skill and dedication. A special thank you to Jo Ann Carey for her clerical support in preparing the catalogue.
- Finally, we want to express our appreciation to our exhibition sponsor Suburban Cable, and to H. F. (Gerry) Lenfest for his personal interest in the exhibition. Gerry Lenfest's deep respect for the art of Barclay Rubincam and other regional artists has grown into a most noteworthy collection that is shared with the employees of The Lenfest Group and Suburban Cable as well as lent to museum exhibitions on a regular basis. We thank Suburban Cable and Gerry Lenfest for their generous support.

Roland H. Woodward, *President and Director*
Chester County Historical Society
August 1998

Lenders to the Exhibition

Mr. and Mrs. W. Whitman Ball

Lydia Willets Bartholomew

Fred T. Cadmus III

Chester County Historical Society

Ann and Alan Clark

Commonwealth Bank

Edward and Jean E. Cotter

Mark and Ghisele Curcio

Mr. and Mrs. Boyd C. Davis

Mr. and Mrs. Ralph L. Easter

Ann and Alex Giorgiani

John and Lisa Hall

Mr. and Mrs. Nicholas Halladay, Sr.

Ann C. Hemphill

Dr. and Mrs. Henry A. Jordan

Gerry Lenfest

Dr. and Mrs. Earl T. Lewis

Mr. and Mrs. George T. Maher

Mrs. Orville R. March

Jean M. Oakes

Ethel L. Reagan

Mrs. Barclay Rubincam

Mr. and Mrs. James C. Sorber

Thomas and Sandra Spackman

William and Elinor Taylor

Mary G. Warden

West Chester University

Penelope P. Wilson

Dr. and Mrs. Harold H. Wingerd, Jr.

Private Collection

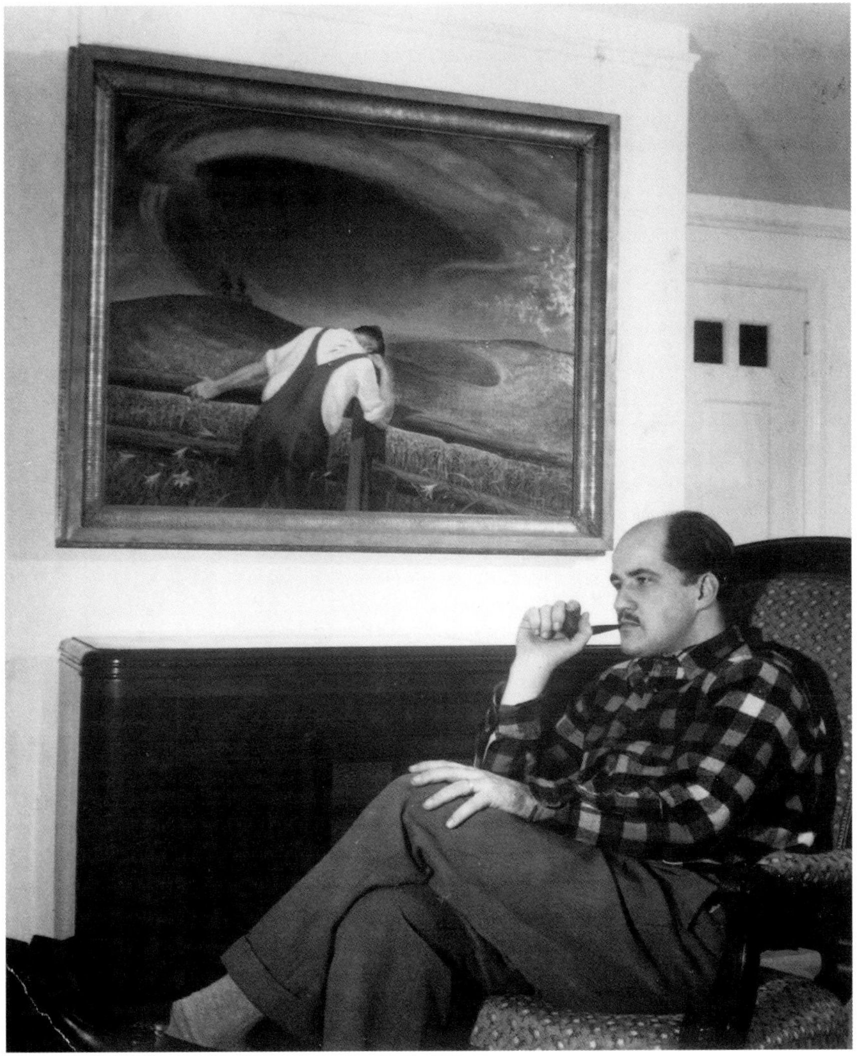

Fig. 1 Barclay Rubincam seated before his painting *Fear Not*, c. 1948

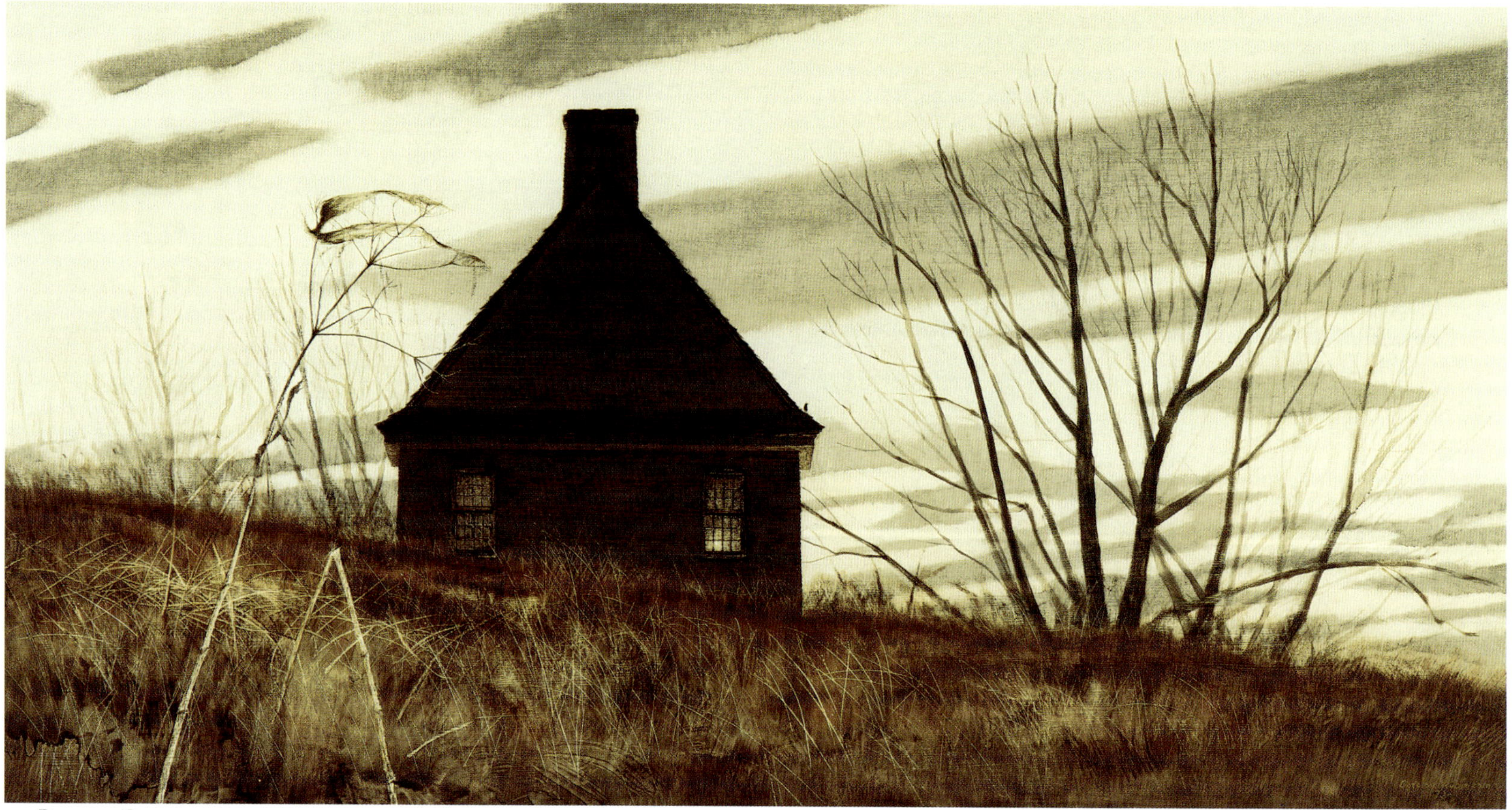

51. Pewter Country

Barclay Rubincam: A Retrospective by Beverly B. Sheppard

The winds of a pewter-colored sky blow through skeletal trees and dry winter grasses. Great gray clouds sweep across an angular hillside. Rising against the curves of sky and land is the silhouette of an eighteenth-century farmhouse. Its strong vertical facade endures the early winter winds, as it has for nearly three centuries. A light in the window offers warmth and shelter.

This is Barclay Rubincam's Chester County, a place where the visual drama of the land is inextricably bound to its history. In Rubincam's art, the terrain of Chester County exceeds geography. The familiar hillsides, rolling farmland and coursing streams are inseparable from the events of the past and the transformation of personal memory. His finest paintings are a composite of history, emotion and the physical beauty of the land he cherished.

Barclay Lawrence Jacob Rubincam (1920-1978), son of Florence and Jacob Rubincam, was born on the family's farm in Newlin Township. His first boyhood home was in the midst of Chester County's pastoral beauty where the west branch of the Brandywine River flows through fields and pasture. The family moved many times during Barclay's childhood, living in Valley Forge, Red Lion, Thorndale and the Unionville area, each setting adding to his visual memories of the land. Growing up, he learned the rhythms and responsibilities of farm life and developed a keen sensitivity to the changing weather patterns and seasonal moods of the countryside. He also exhibited an early interest in art and spent many childhood hours sketching and painting. The landscape around him was a frequent topic.

Art was central to his school life as well. Years later Barclay would tell his wife Caroline Hannum Rubincam that he was perhaps too often excused from classes to paint murals or posters or draw holiday decorations. He was permitted to substitute art projects for academic assignments, creating an accurate model of the Globe Theater, for example, rather than writing a paper about Shakespeare. His talents were indulged, and his school experience reinforced his love of art.

Following graduation from Unionville High School, Barclay enrolled in the Wilmington Academy of Fine Art, which offered a rigorous five-day-a-week curriculum. His teachers included Frank Schoonover, Gayle Hoskins and N.C. Wyeth, artists influenced by the illustrations and techniques of Howard Pyle. It is probable that his instructors shared Pyle's teachings with Barclay, especially an interest in research and accuracy in historical detail.

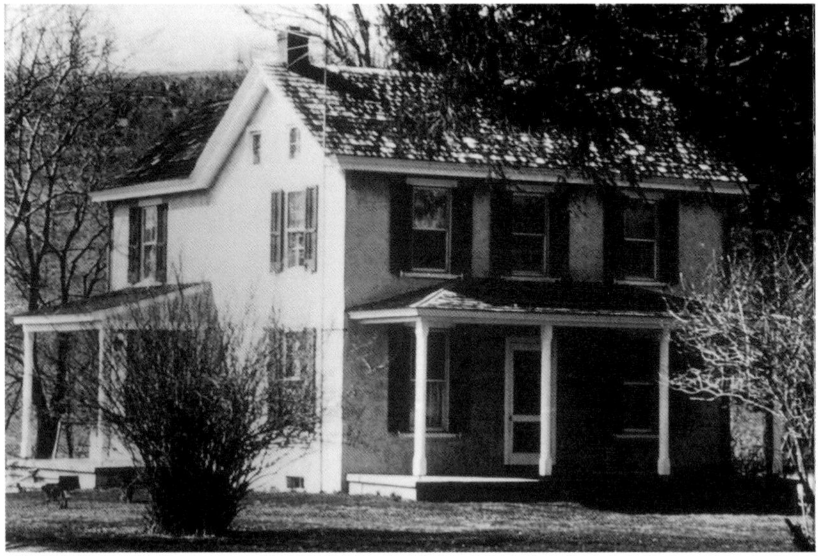

Fig. 2 Birthplace of both Barclay and his father in Newlin Township, Chester County

The young artist came to the attention of the local newspapers at this time. An article in West Chester's *Daily Local News* (August 15, 1940) describes a view of West Chester composed by Rubincam from a vantage point atop the Warner Theater. He worked as an usher in the theater's balcony section and also earned a dollar a week to change the theater's marquee. Perhaps the view from his ladder inspired his aerial composition. The painting may have been the beginning of Rubincam's lifelong interest in illustrating both the architecture and history of the county seat.

World War II interrupted Barclay's education. In June 1942, he was drafted and sent to New Caledonia in the South Pacific with an engineering unit. Typically, he filled many hours sketching his new surroundings and his fellow soldiers, giving them drawings to send back home. The Army was in need of an illustrator and muralist, and Barclay was reassigned as a section artist, attached to the Information Education Section of the South Pacific Command in New Caledonia. He was promoted to staff sergeant, given his own apartment and spent the next three years continuing the work he loved.

Rubincam created art with energy and passion in New Caledonia. His portraits of both local residents and Army friends are strong and vigorous and reveal the friendships he established. His sketches and paintings record a landscape very different from his native Chester County and show his grasp of the unique detail and brilliant color of the region. He also painted posters and murals for the Army, and an article in the *Daily Local News* (August 5, 1943) describes murals depicting a panoramic history of freedom "which adorns the walls of the office of Major General Rush B. Lincoln of Washington, D.C. and Ames, Iowa."

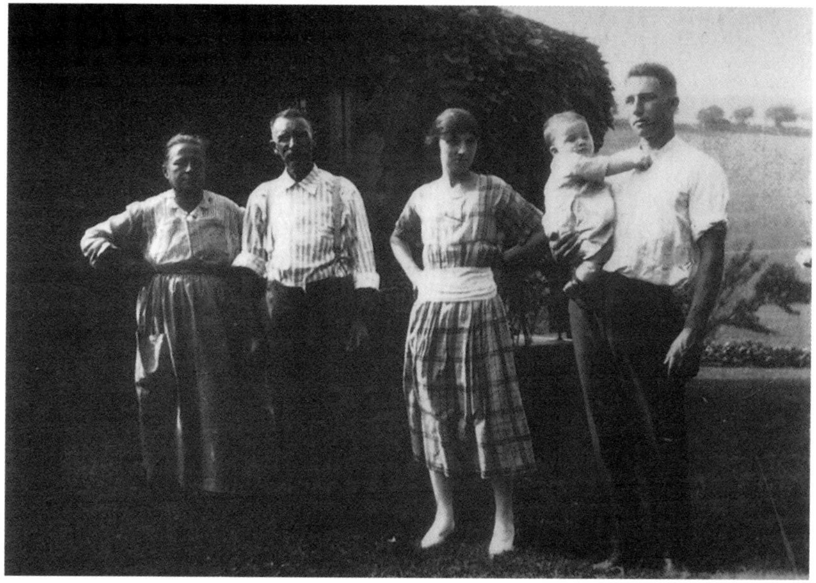

Fig. 3 Barclay with his parents and grandparents, c. 1921

N.C. Wyeth had written to Barclay during the war, and Rubincam expected to complete his education with Wyeth in Chadds Ford and at Wilmington when he came home. His plans were changed by Wyeth's tragic death in 1945, and Barclay never returned to school. After a brief move to Plainfield, New Jersey, he returned to West Chester where he opened a studio, advertising that he did "Portraiture, Mural Decoration, Lettering and Layout." In September 1946, Barclay married Caroline Hannum and soon after settled into a home on North New Street, making West Chester his permanent residence.

Rubincam was a disciplined worker. His widow describes a typical day as beginning early in the morning in the garden, where his interests in gardening and landscaping paralleled his artistic attention to composition and design. Even in the garden he planned carefully, using a chalkstring and yardstick to lay out his plantings. Following a "hearty" breakfast, he either went out to sketch or into the studio to paint. Though he took a lunch break, he returned to work immediately afterward. He often had more than one project going – frequently a pastel and an oil painting, so he could keep working while the oil paint dried.

He never abandoned a work, according to Caroline, finishing every painting and project no matter how tedious it might be. He was a skillful craftsman, designing and building the cabinetry and woodwork in their home and applying a perfectionist's approach even to the arrangement of household

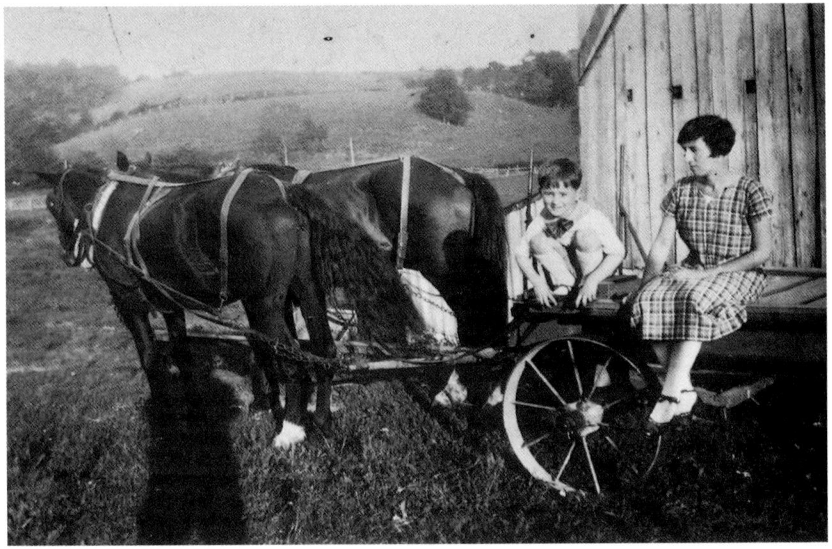

Fig. 4 Young Barclay and his mother, 1927

furniture, art and antiques. He trusted his eye for design, and when he completed a painting, he brought it into the living room to hang for a few days so that he could study it carefully and be sure details of color and composition were correct.

Barclay prepared carefully for each painting, often making numerous sketches. Much of his preliminary work for landscapes was done on site, and he frequently noted the location of a subject on the back of the painting. On the reverse of *Late Afternoon on Brandywine Battlefield* [Cat. 53], for example, he wrote, "Field across from Mr. and Mrs. John Hall, Birmingham, Chester County, PA." Similarly, the painting *After the Rain* [Cat. 32] is further identified as "Sykes Farm at Rte. 842 and the Brandywine." Occasionally, he provided information about related work on a topic. A label on the back of one landscape [Cat. 44] notes, "Pencil sketch on location. This was sketched on the old Brinton Farm – Chester County. An oil painted of this and a pastel –"

Preparation was key to Rubincam's history paintings as well. Caroline Rubincam spent long hours at the Chester County Historical Society researching a variety of topics. Barclay consulted the photographic collection of Ashton B. T. Smith, Sr. for views of early West Chester and drew inspiration from such sources as the nineteenth-century publication, *A History of Chester County, Pennsylvania*, written by J. Smith Futhey and Gilbert Cope. He cites information on page 117 in Futhey and Cope as the background for his painting *Uplanders at the New Court House* [Cat. 10]. His highly popular painting *Looking North on High Street* [Cat. 7], commissioned by John Hall of the Chester County Federal Savings and Loan, is based on a sketch in Futhey and Cope attributed to an earlier publication on Pennsylvania history.

Barclay's fascination with the past was recognized in 1947 when local newspapers reported that the young artist had composed an historical map of Turk's Head (West Chester) and found it highly appropriate for the town's one hundred and fiftieth anniversary to be celebrated in 1949. A *Daily Local News* article (April 23, 1947) referred to the map as "a lesson in local history," complete with such symbols of the region's past as a cream separator, wagon wheel, air compressor and diploma – all referring to local industries and institutions. It included ten vignettes of "historic shrines" and biographical sketches of two notable citizens.

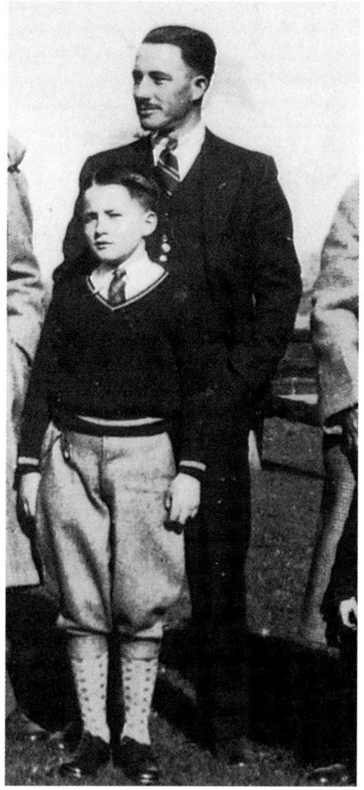

Fig. 5 Barclay with his father Jacob, 1931

Understanding the popular appeal of local history, Barclay designed three additional maps, the Battle of Brandywine, the Valley Forge Encampment and the Battle of Gettysburg, all of which were reproduced and sold locally. Rubincam sent a copy of the map of the Battle of Brandywine, created for the 170th anniversary (1947) of the event, to President Truman and received an appreciation from the President.

Each map reflected Barclay's great enthusiasm and factual grasp of the history he portrayed. His sister Barbara, twenty-one years younger than her artist brother, recalls his remarkable knowledge of the Civil War. In 1953, as a special treat for her twelfth birthday, Barclay took Barbara to Gettysburg, walking the battlefield with her. Today she continues to cite that experience as the one that stimulated her lifelong interest in Civil War history.

From the late 1940s on, Rubincam exhibited his work frequently in juried and non-juried regional shows and built a close association with the Chester County Art Association. Several paintings exhibited locally drew the attention of major museums. *Ring of Autumn* [Cat. 6] appeared in the 143rd Annual Exhibition of the Pennsylvania Academy of the Fine Arts in 1948 and traveled from there to the Toledo Museum of Art. *I Believe* was purchased by the Pennsylvania Academy of Fine Arts and is one of many Rubincam paintings in the permanent collections of such institutions as the Brandywine River Museum and the Chester County Historical Society. The majority of Rubincam paintings continue to be owned in Chester County by both private owners and local institutions. Caroline Rubincam has expressed Barclay's deep pleasure in sharing his work with friends, noting that he preferred that they consider the paintings "cherished possessions" rather than investments.

Rubincam did not have a gallery that sold his work. Most of his sales were handled personally, though he often exhibited paintings at the Village Flower Shop owned by Bob and Henry Guss. They would place a painting in the window, where it might catch the eye of a passing lawyer or businessman. Most portraits and a few landscapes were commissioned, but Barclay preferred the artistic freedom of selecting his own topics and interpretations. Selling art was his only income, however, and he kept track of requests for specific landmarks and styles. He understood the popularity of references to the county's colonial roots, the American Revolution and the colorful moments in West Chester's past.

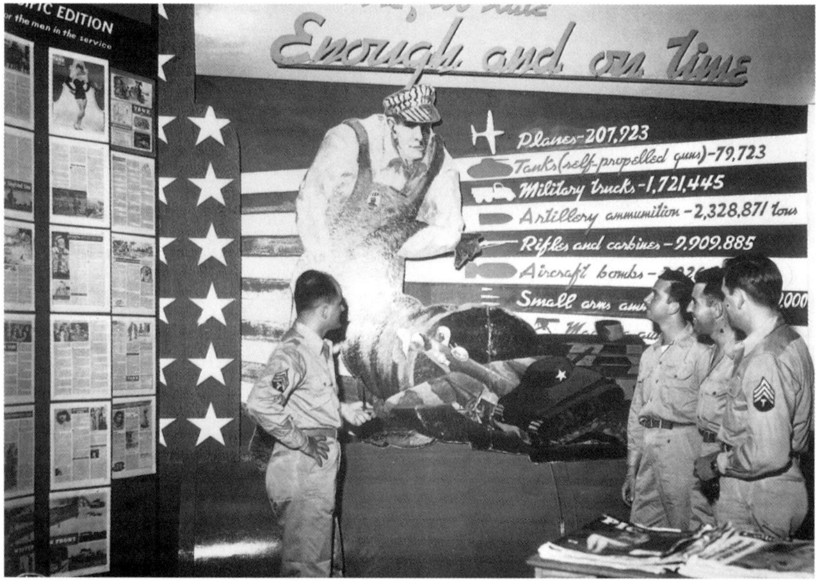

Fig. 6 Photograph of Rubincam with wartime mural during service in the South Pacific Command in New Caledonia (1942–1945)

Shadows of the past extend across many Rubincam paintings. Whether still life, historical narrative, landscape or portraiture, they share a sense of time compressed. His friend Chris Sanderson, a remarkable collector, historian and recounter of the past, was once referred to as "a living link to all the memorable dates, places, and events which comprised America's coming of age." In many ways, Barclay infused his paintings with a similar spirit.

This parallel role is suggested in the painting *Jefferis Ford, Sept. 11, 1777* [Cat. 18]. The figure of Sanderson stands in the shadow of an enormous tree, perhaps one of the "Penn Oaks" that witnessed the arrival of William Penn to Chester County. In the distance, red-coated British troops cross the Brandywine in a tactical move that would eventually lead to Washington's defeat at the Battle of Brandywine. The events occur in the foggy distance of time, and Sanderson looks back at the viewer as if he is the narrator of the past. Barclay, like Chris, often played a similar role – tying the past to the present by placing time's shadows into the context of today.

Rubincam employed a number of pictorial devices to fuse time and place. Some historical topics were simply depicted in the past. West Chester at the turn of the century, for example, was illustrated at a specific historical moment. Another technique was to include a composite of details from different periods. In his portraits, Barclay often surrounded his subjects with various images from their personal histories. He revealed the history in the landscape through such visible reminders as eighteenth-century buildings, covered bridges, barns and historic farms nestled in the hollows of the fields. At times, he suggested age in the worn facade of a familiar building, the contrast of old and new, or the stillness of a moment that seems frozen in time.

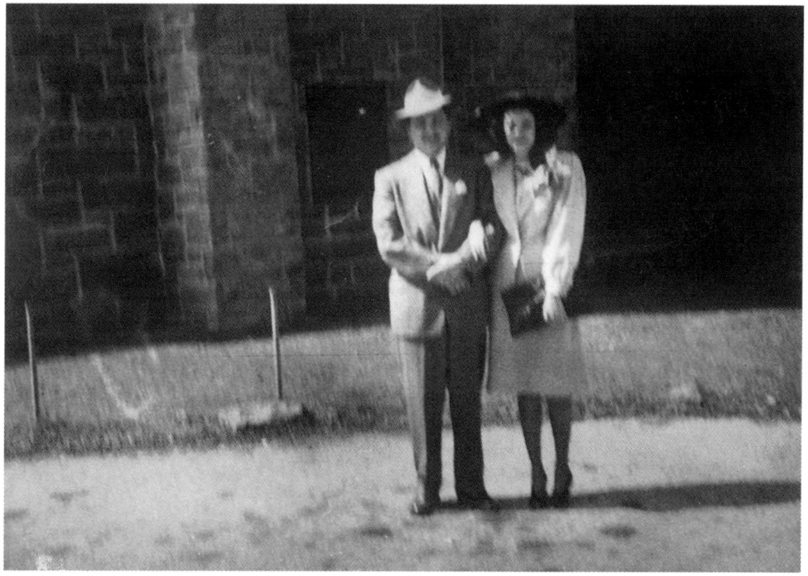

Fig. 7 Wedding day photograph of Barclay and Caroline Hannum Rubincam, 1946

One of the most stunning reminders of the persistence of history is the literal appearance of a shadow out of time across the evening facade of Birmingham Meeting in the painting *Sentry at Birmingham* [Cat. 17]. The meetinghouse stood in the midst of the Battle of Brandywine as the fighting raged between British and Continental soldiers. Later it served as a hospital for wounded British soldiers. Fallen soldiers from both armies are buried there in a common grave. The meetinghouse remains an active place of worship today, its solemn exterior a visible statement of Quaker simplicity.

Rubincam's treatment of the building's facade, emphasizing the massive strength of each stone and the clarity of its architectural features, presents an image of endurance. The shadow of a Revolutionary-era soldier is ghostlike in comparison, but powerful in its reminder of a dramatic past. A comparison of the study [Cat. 16] for the painting with the finished version shows the artist's eye in formulating a strong composition. He lowers the horizontal eave at the top, paralleling the picture plane and reinforcing the stillness of the moment. He enlarges the window to the left, adding more lines to the vertical-horizontal grid of the facade. He alters the shadow of the sentry as well, changing the angle of the tri-cornered hat to counter the rigidity of the background grid. The eerie sway of shadowed branches animates the mood.

Among Rubincam's most powerful compositions, are the still life paintings *Generations* [Cat. 56] and *It's Raining* [Cat. 59], both painted in the early 1950s. Each bears a similarity to *Sentry at Birmingham* in the power of contrasting the strength and endurance of architecture against the life forces of nature. The implications of history are seen in the worn facades of the structures, the overhanging roof of a timber barn and the cracked stucco of the side of the house. In *Generations*, the branches of a young tree echo the lines in the fractured stucco, offering a contrast between old and new. *It's Raining* uses a daring compositional device: a strong vertical line, the edge of the barn, cuts directly through the center of the painting. Rubincam offsets its thrust with the thick, dark diagonal shape of the overhanging roof. The geometry of both lines contrasts with the twisting branches of a large tree and the softness of the falling rain. The influence of N.C. Wyeth, a master of composition, is seen in many of these early still life paintings.

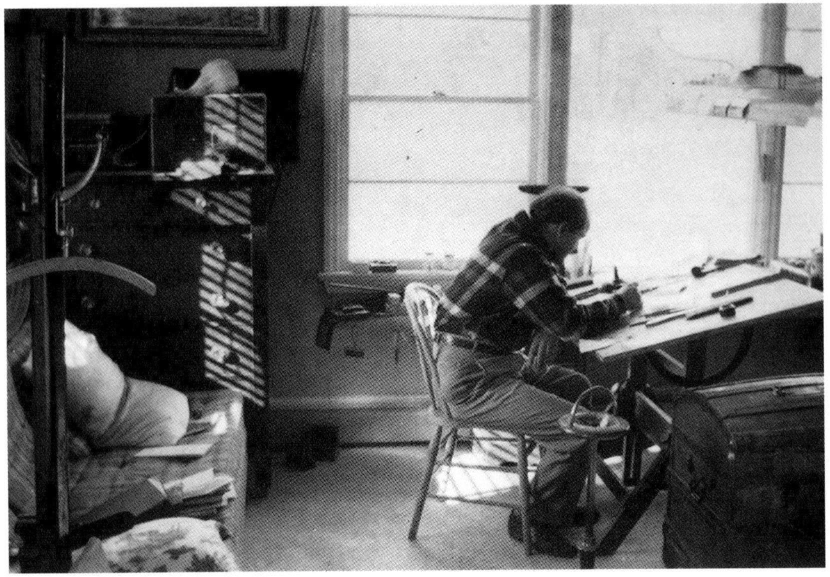

Fig. 8 Rubincam at work in his studio, Thanksgiving, 1948

Although Barclay's formal art education was brief, his work suggests a number of possible influences. In subject matter and passion for Chester County, he reflects the enduring American interest in regionalism. Across the country artists were painting scenes and events typical of their sections of America, employing clear, realistic styles to portray images that could be enjoyed by all. One of his student paintings, *Spring Plowing 1940* [Cat. 1], bears a strong stylistic relationship to the work of Thomas Hart Benton, a painter much respected by Barclay. The seasonal rhythms of agrarian life are expressed in lines that echo the contours of the land.

Early Morning in January [Cat. 40] invites comparison to Winslow Homer's *The Fox Hunt*. Each portrays the fury of crows in pursuit of a fleeing fox. The use of strong diagonals intensifies the drama of the moment. Barclay presents the encounter from the bird's-eye view. The fox runs far below, and the impact of the painting is in the bold shape of the black birds. In contrast, Homer places the viewer on the level of the fox in the moment before the savage attack. Our empathy is clearly with the fox, whereas with Barclay, we are more drawn to admiration of the powerful birds.

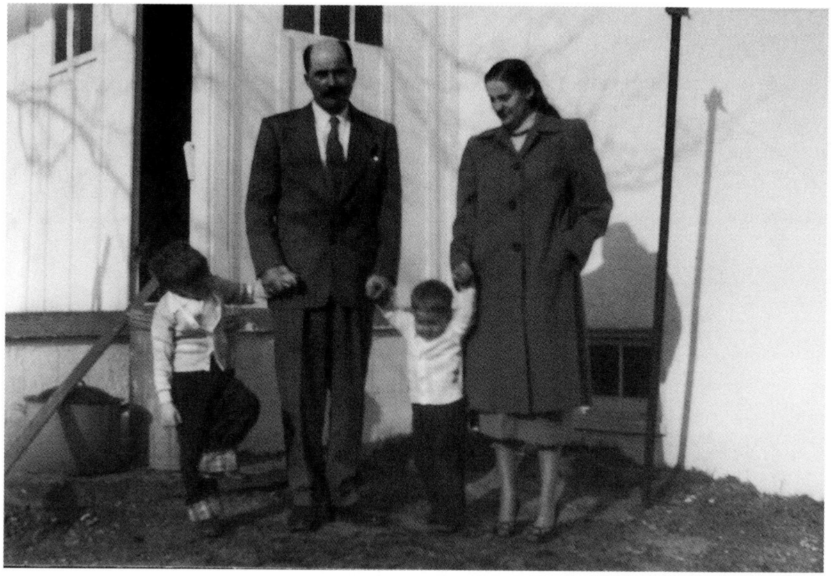

Fig. 9 Barclay and Caroline Rubincam, with sons André (l.) and Reginald (r.), c. 1955

Study with Schoonover, Wyeth and Hoskins shared aspects of the art of illustration that may also have influenced Rubincam's work. One particularly valuable lesson was the need to be familiar with historical details, such as dress, architecture, social habits, and technology, in order to depict believable scenes. Though Barclay was never an illustrator as such, he understood this lesson as it applied to his history paintings. One reason for their popularity may have been the thoroughness of his preparation.

The views of early West Chester are filled with numerous period details, including a stunning array of early vehicles, such as Conestoga wagons, trolleys, bicycles, milk wagons and a variety of carts and horses. Several early buildings, including the Green Tree Inn, the Turk's Head Inn, the 1786 Courthouse, the Hemphill Building and the Bank of Chester County are accurately positioned and rendered with attention to architectural detail. Aspects of clothing, accessories, activity and mannerisms required research as well. In a whimsical gesture, Barclay also included a self-portrait in each West Chester scene – the mustachioed policeman, newspaper reader or casual observer – suggesting his firsthand presence in the past.

While working on *Sentry at Birmingham*, Barclay exhibited another aspect of his insistence on accuracy. He used a neighbor as a model for the sentry, outlining his figure against the garage wall during daytime hours. At night he carried a lantern to the meetinghouse to make certain the shadows were accurate. Similarly, he studied photographs and even interviewed a trolley driver before completing his painting of turn-of-the-century West Chester.

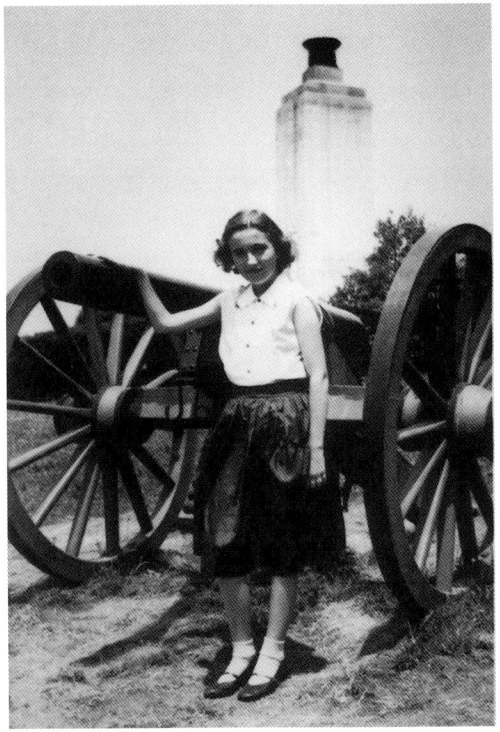

Fig. 10 Barclay's photograph of his sister Barbara, taken at Gettysburg in 1953

The details of uniforms and the sequence of events are also carefully presented in his paintings of the American Revolution. *The Revolutionary War Hospital at Yellow Springs* [Cat. 25] provides an excellent example. The painting shows a stone foundation surmounted by a frame building still under construction, even though the hospital is in use. During the winter of the Valley Forge encampment, when sickness ravaged the camp, the hospital was filled long before it was finished. The painting shows a dead soldier being carried from the building even as more of the sick arrive. A cart filled with straw is an ominous sight. The straw became the patient's bedding and frequently spread disease from soldier to soldier. Rubincam's painting is narrative. The drama is not contrived; it is the drama of reality.

Despite the popularity of the history paintings, many admire Rubincam most for the beauty of his landscapes that expressed the essence of Chester County. Through his brush, the familiar contour of the land, the wooded hillsides, open fields and meandering curves of the Brandywine River offer endless views and changing moods. Nostalgia is often a central theme. *Boys Along the Brandywine* [Cat. 39] is a bucolic idyll – fresh, green and cool as two young boys with fishing poles walk beside the languorous flow of the river. *Memories of Our Farm* [Cat. 54] incorporates memory into a composite visual story. The fine stone home and outbuildings, flowering trees, geese on a pond, small log house in the background, the family car in the driveway, a tractor, lazy cows, a running dog and a zigzag of geese reappear from the past to capture the essence of the Orville March farm of earlier days.

Caroline Rubincam recalls how Barclay's boyhood days on a farm taught him great sensitivity to seasonal changes and weather patterns. Subtle shifts in light and atmosphere soften or sharpen each view. *Moonlight on the Brandywine* [Cat. 43] glows with suffused light. Distant trees blend into a twilight gray lit only by moonlight and the delicacy of fireflies. Darkness also intensifies the patterns of *Sconnelltown Hill* [Cat. 55] where a remarkable range of blues, blacks and muted whites create a patchwork of patterns along the river's nighttime banks. The snow-covered ground is background to the graceful architecture of trees and the etched boundaries of distant farms.

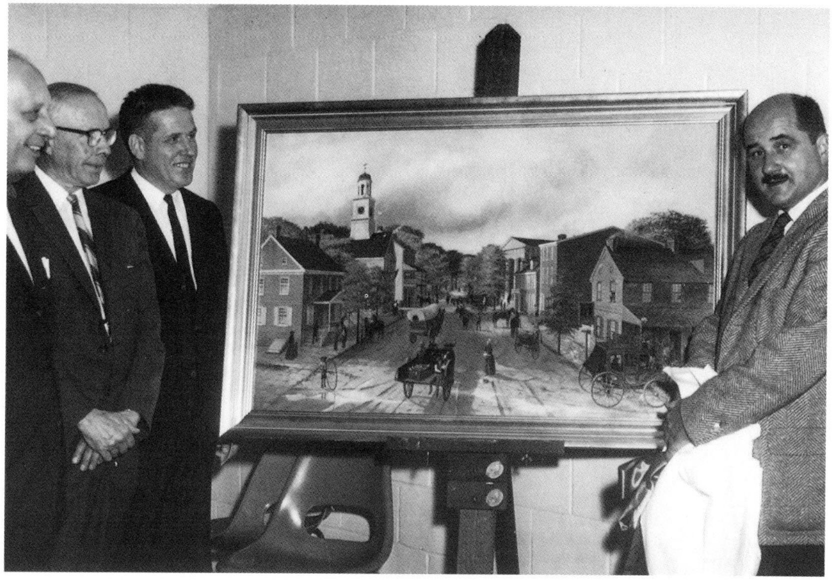

Fig. 11 The unveiling of *Looking North on High Street*, commissioned by the Chester County Federal Savings and Loan, September 1963. Pictured, left to right, are George Andrews, Arthur James, John Hall and Barclay

Mood also prevails in *July Storm* [Cat. 48] where fields of waist-high grains already bend in the wind as a blackened sky advances. In *From the Car Window* [Cat. 47] hundreds of startled blackbirds rise from a dry field. The shadow of the car strikes an eerie note, perhaps portending the encroachment of development. *Fireworks – Fourth of July Looking Out Over Lenape* [Cat. 50] sets an altogether different tone as the viewer joins a group of onlookers, figures silhouetted against the darkness. The mood is inviting as we watch the rows of car lights moving along the roads below and the delicate lights of fireworks in the sky above.

Rubincam's untimely death in 1978 interrupted a career dedicated to preserving Chester County's history and beauty on canvas. A gregarious man who enjoyed his many friendships and liked nothing better than an evening of conversation, Rubincam was deeply missed by friends, family and many distant admirers. His work, however, continues to share the joy he found in the richness of his home territory.

Barclay Rubincam's Chester County is a familiar place. The landmarks are well known, and the configuration of the land distinctive. The image of the Brandywine River flowing through meadows and rocky pastures is at its core. The early history of this land is legend, and its remnants are visible across the hillsides. Like the artist Carolyn Wyeth who once said, "All I want is the same old thing. . . . I know it so well," Barclay never tired of his subject matter. Its luster never dimmed, and in his fusion of beauty and history, he made the familiar a subject of enduring substance.

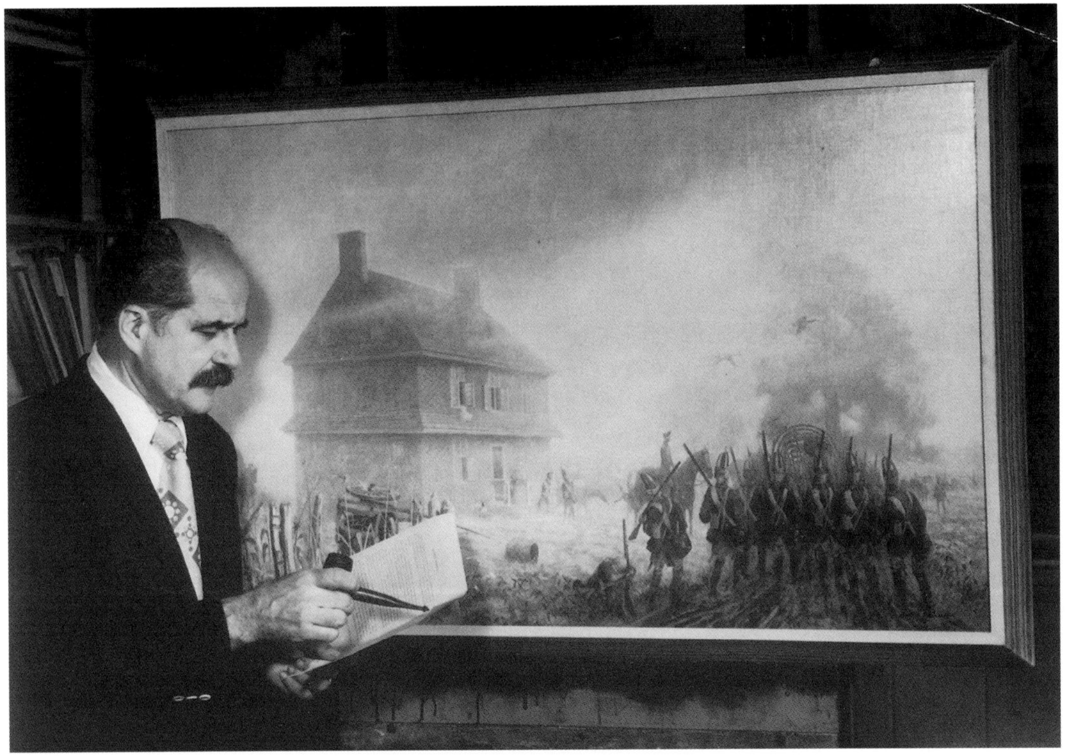

Fig. 12 Barclay with painting of the Barns-Brinton House, featured in a 1977 exhibition in Yellow Springs

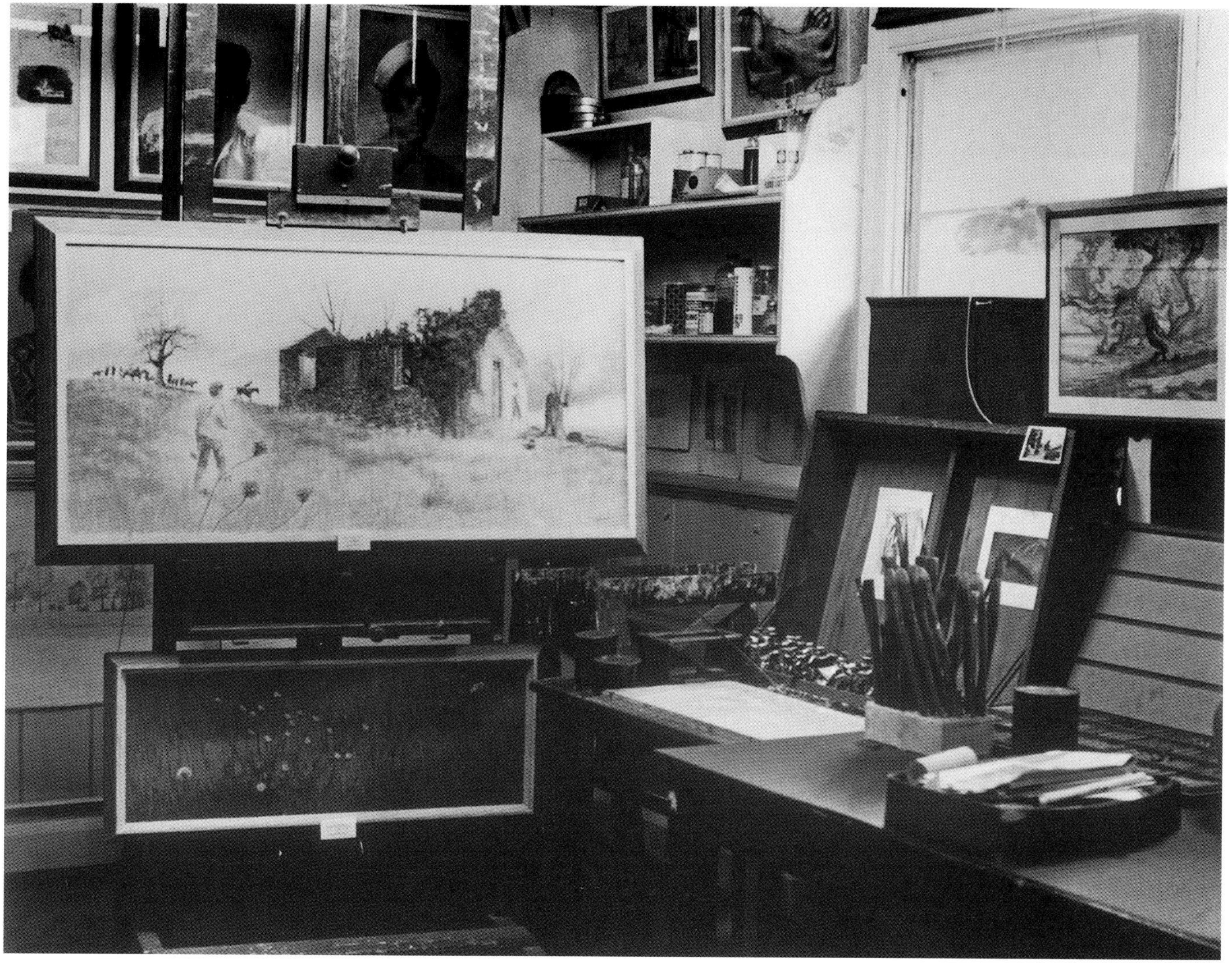

Fig. 13 Rubincam's studio in his home on North New Street, 1978

Early Work

Rubincam's earliest work reveals an affinity with American regionalism through his embrace of realism and his interest in local themes. Whether documenting the history and landscape of Chester County or illustrating the people and places of New Caledonia, Rubincam demonstrated keen observational skills, an eye for essential detail and a passion for capturing the visual essence of life around him.

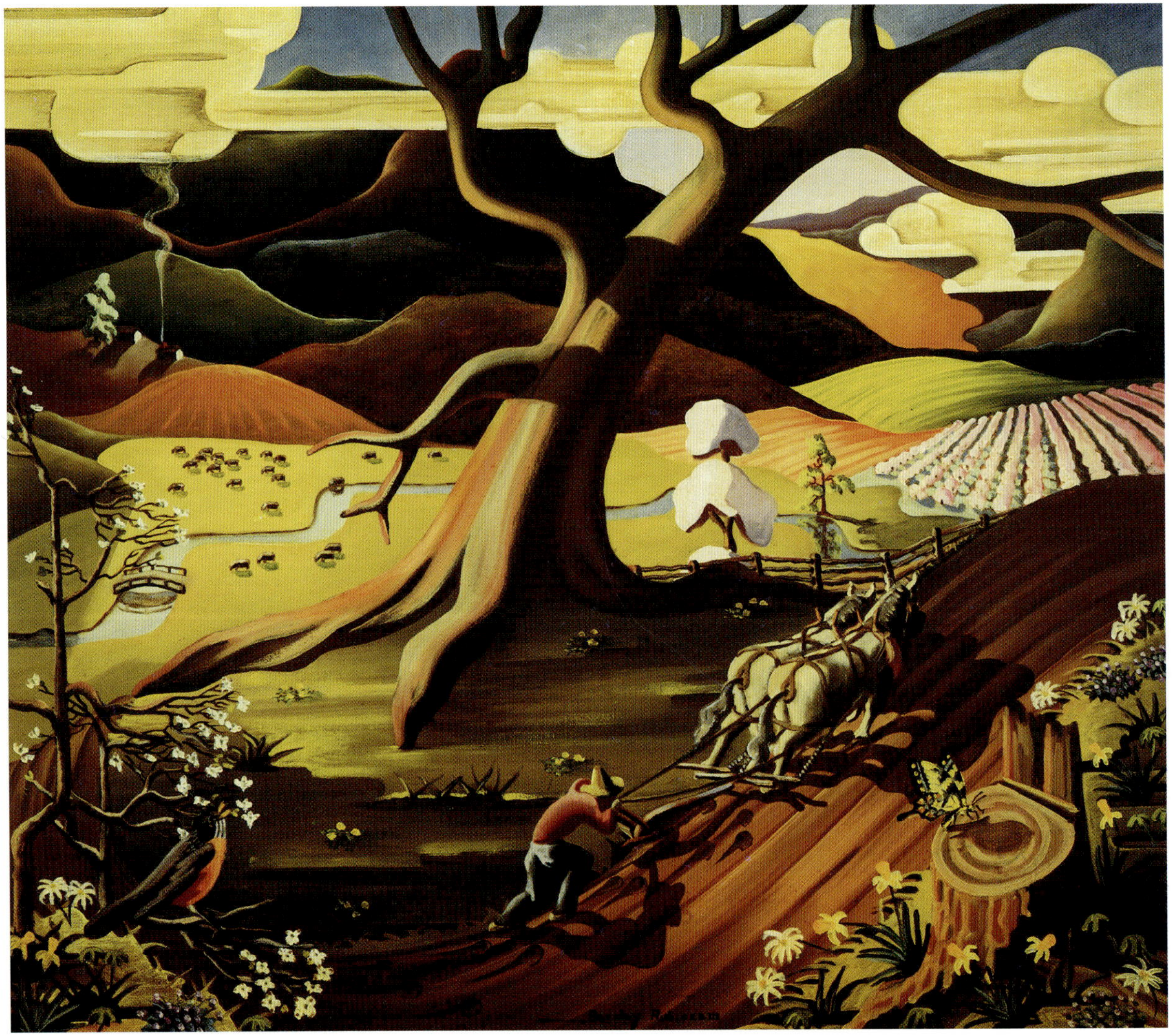

1. Spring Plowing, 1940

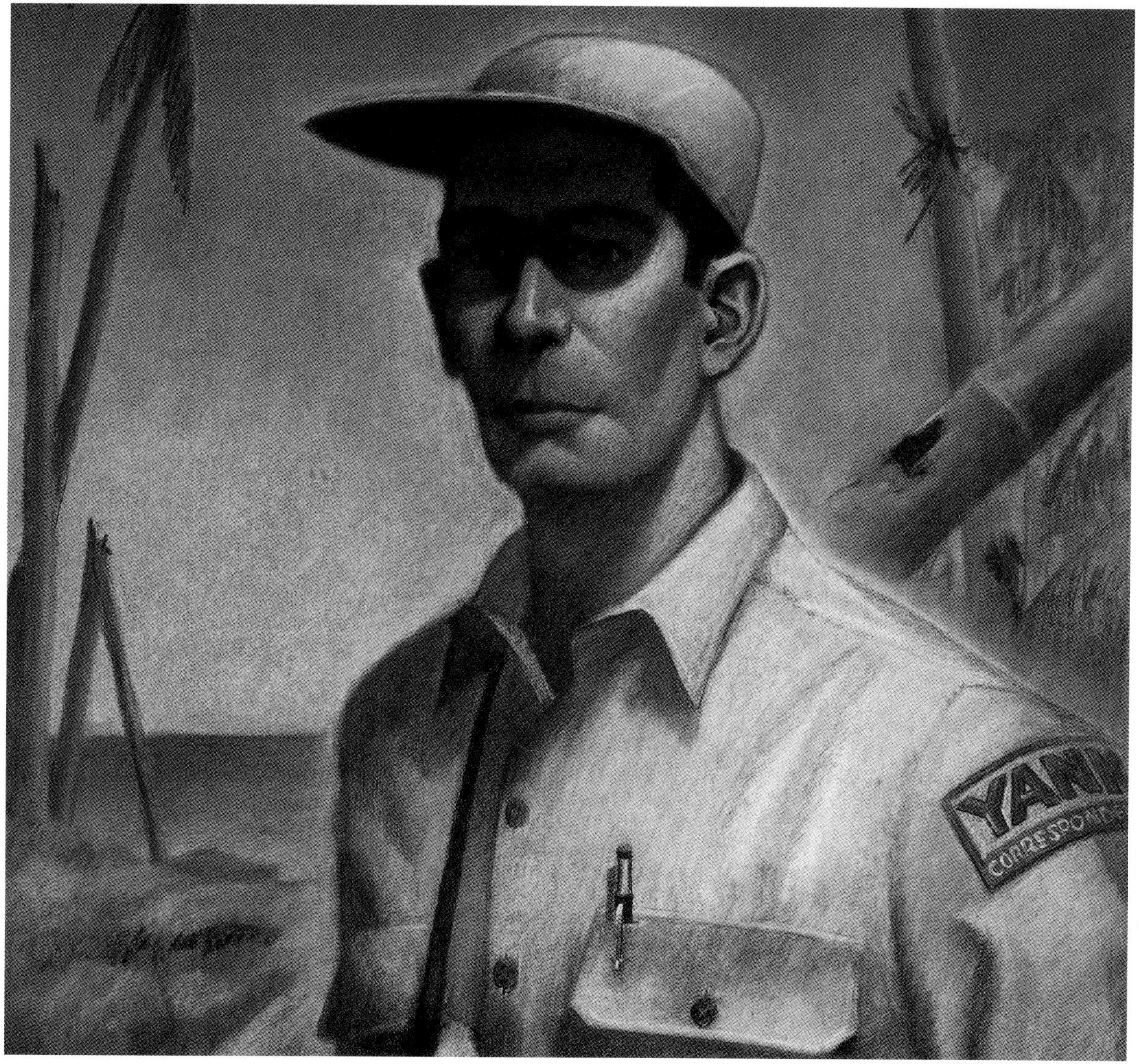

2. Yank Correspondent

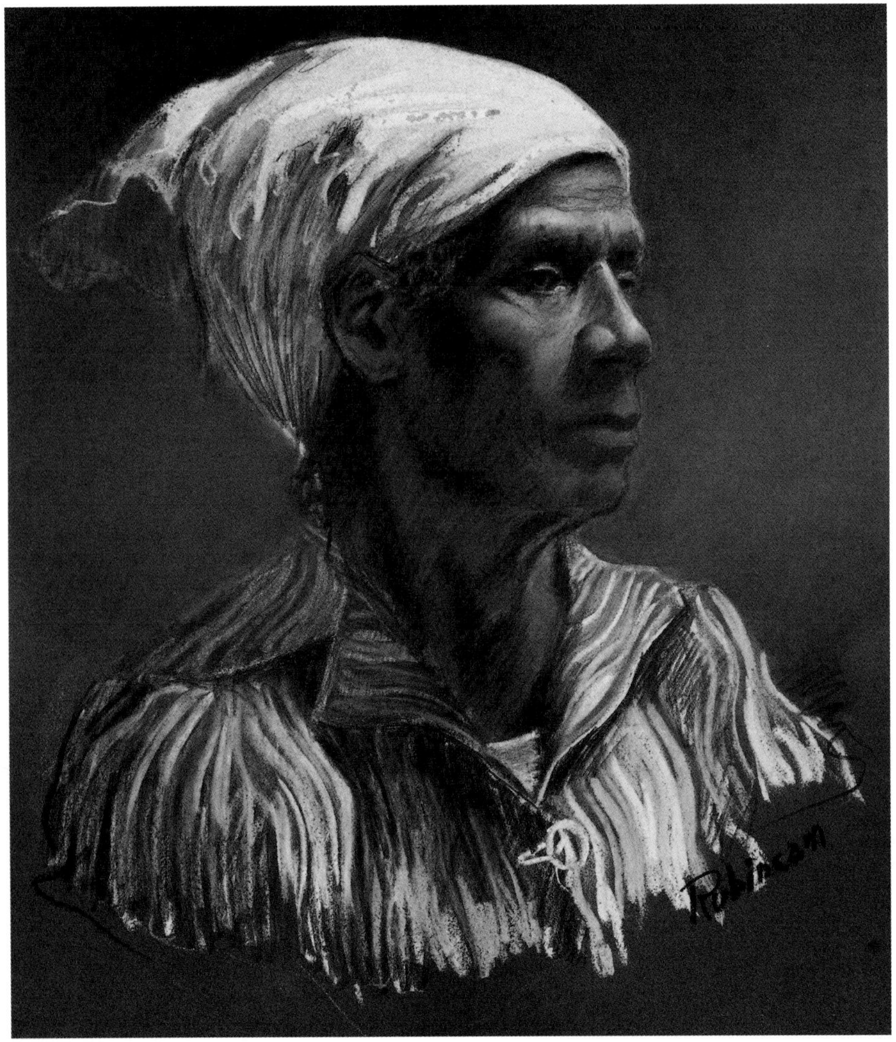

3. Kanaka Mother in
White Turban

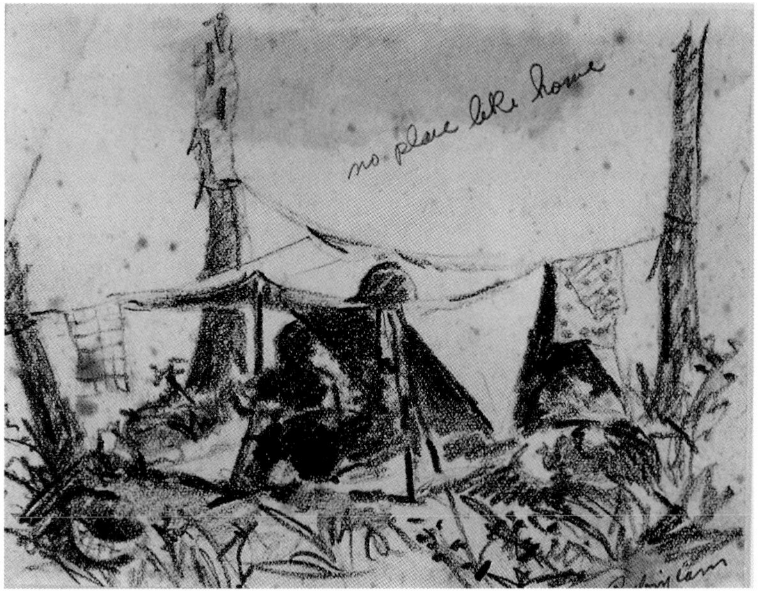

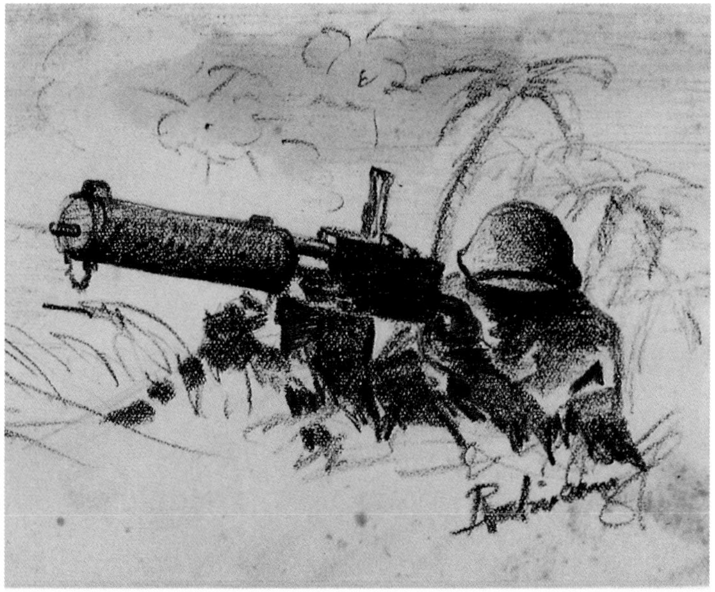

4. Sketches from New Caledonia

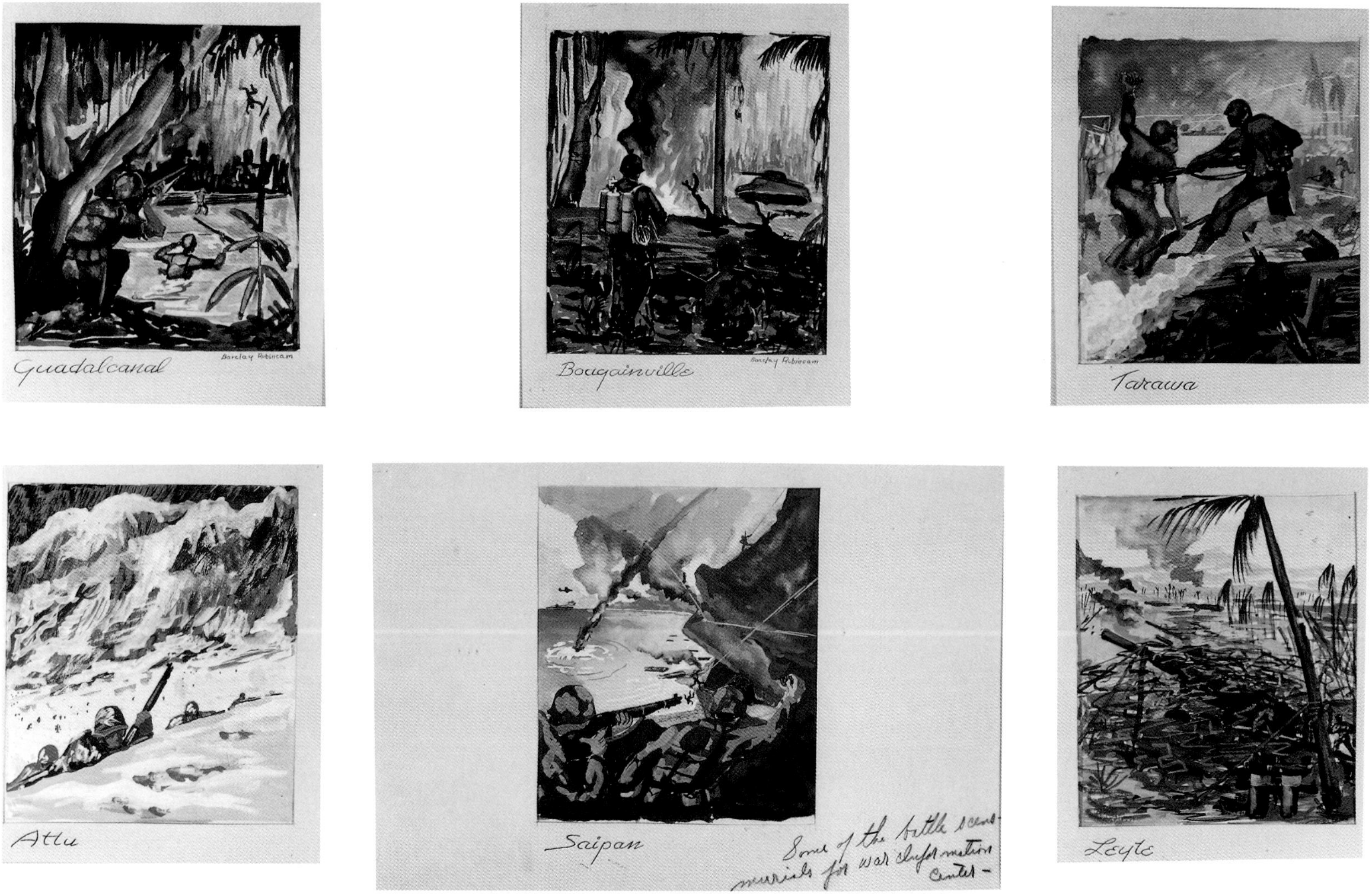

5. Sketches for Battle Scene Murals for War Information Center

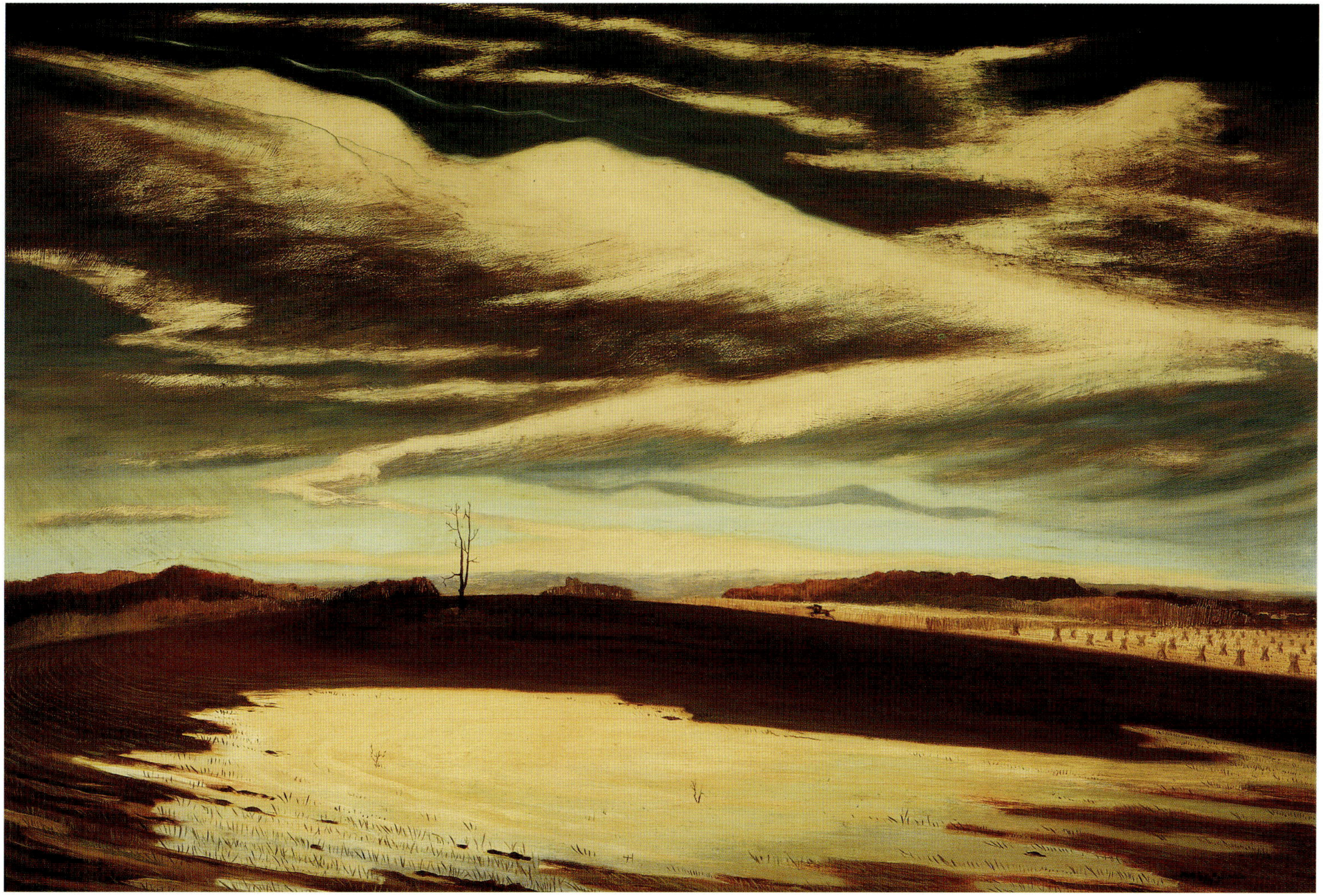

6. Ring of Autumn

West Chester History

West Chester's colorful history fascinated Barclay Rubincam. Inspired by turn-of-the-century photographs and early sketches, he illustrated many moments in the borough's past, covering more than a century of growth and change. He often focused on the intersection at High and Market Streets, historically the center of town and the site of the famed Turk's Head Inn, which gave the town its first name. Rubincam's West Chester is a place of charm and story, filled with life and free of blemish.

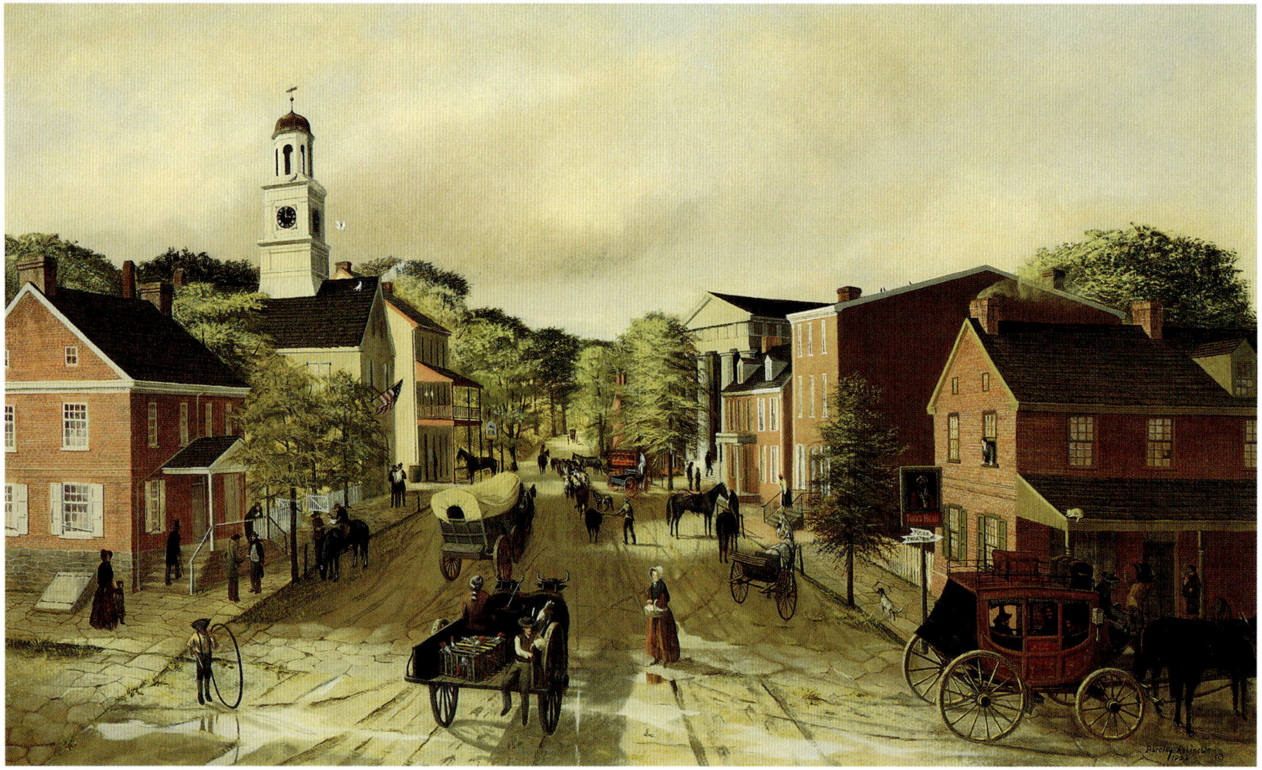

7. Looking North on High Street

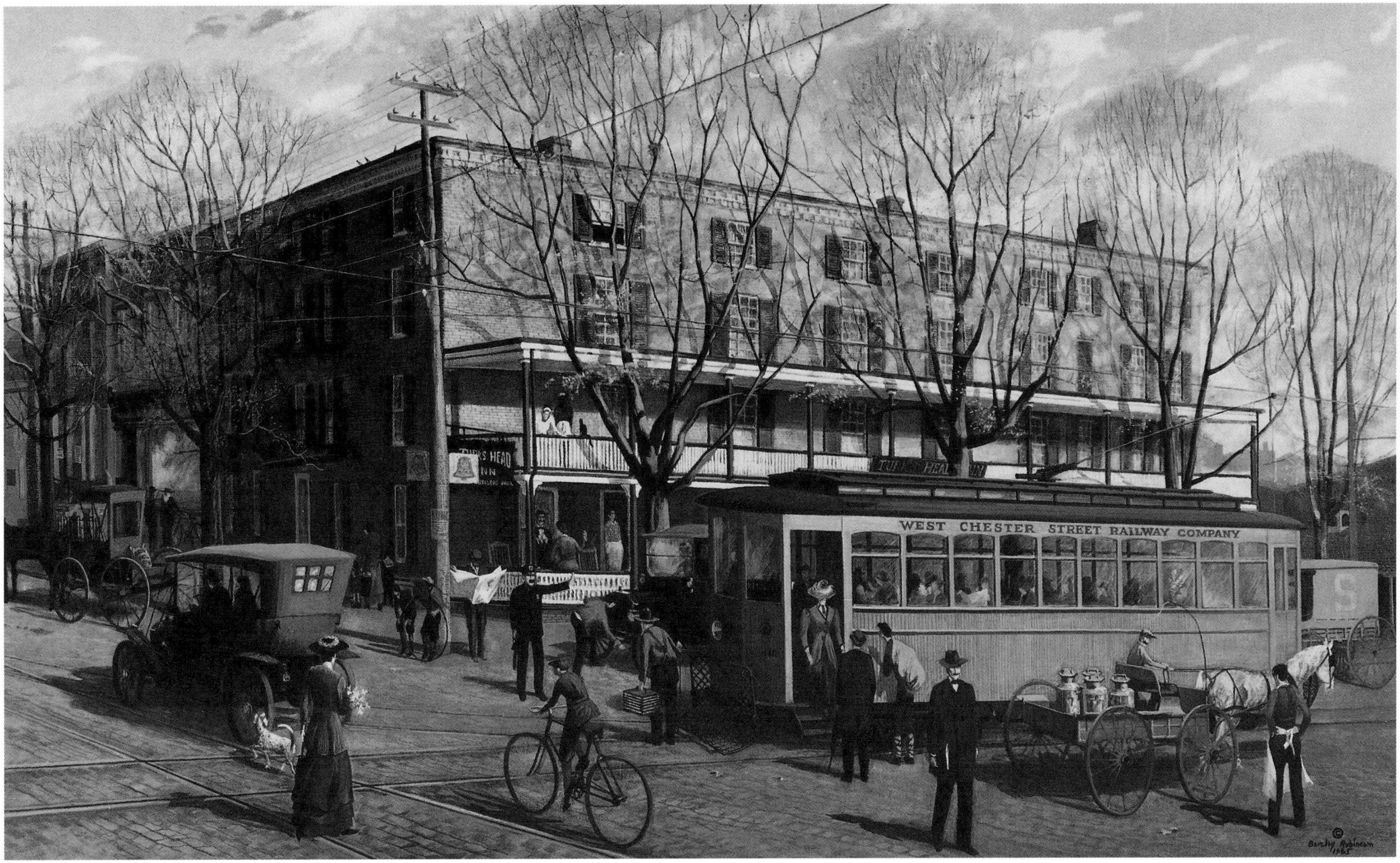

8. At the Turn of the Century

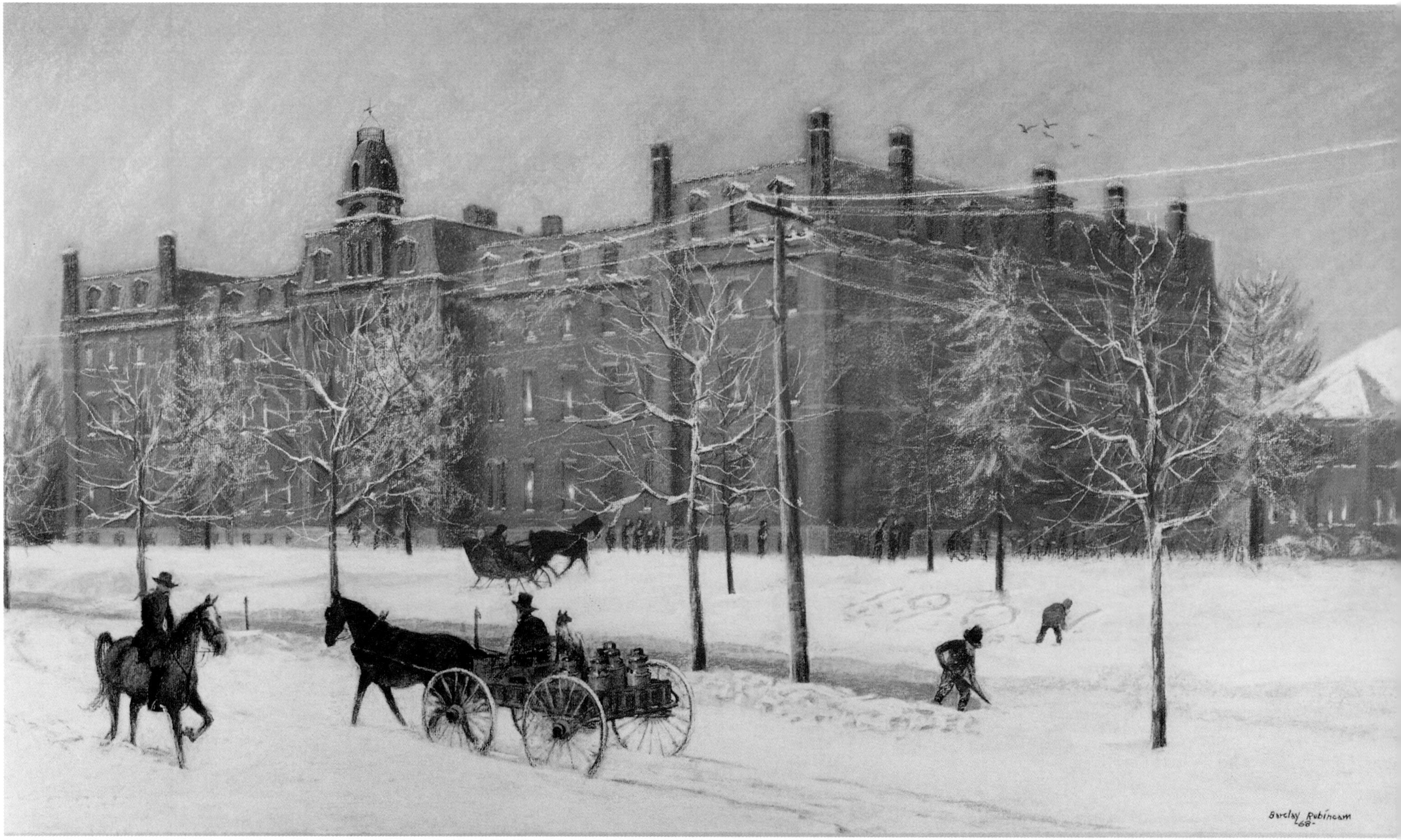

9. Old Main

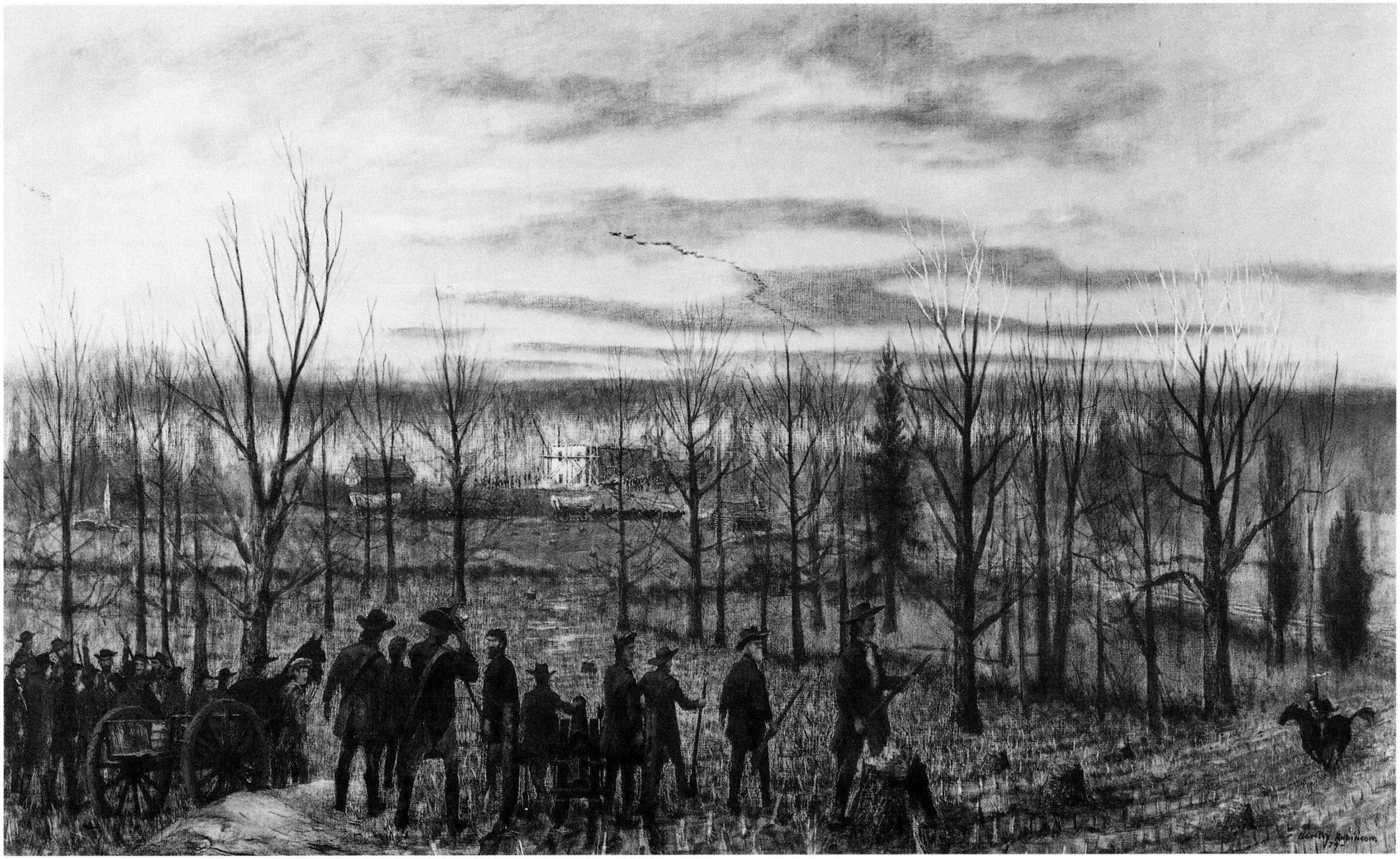

10. Uplanders at the New Court House

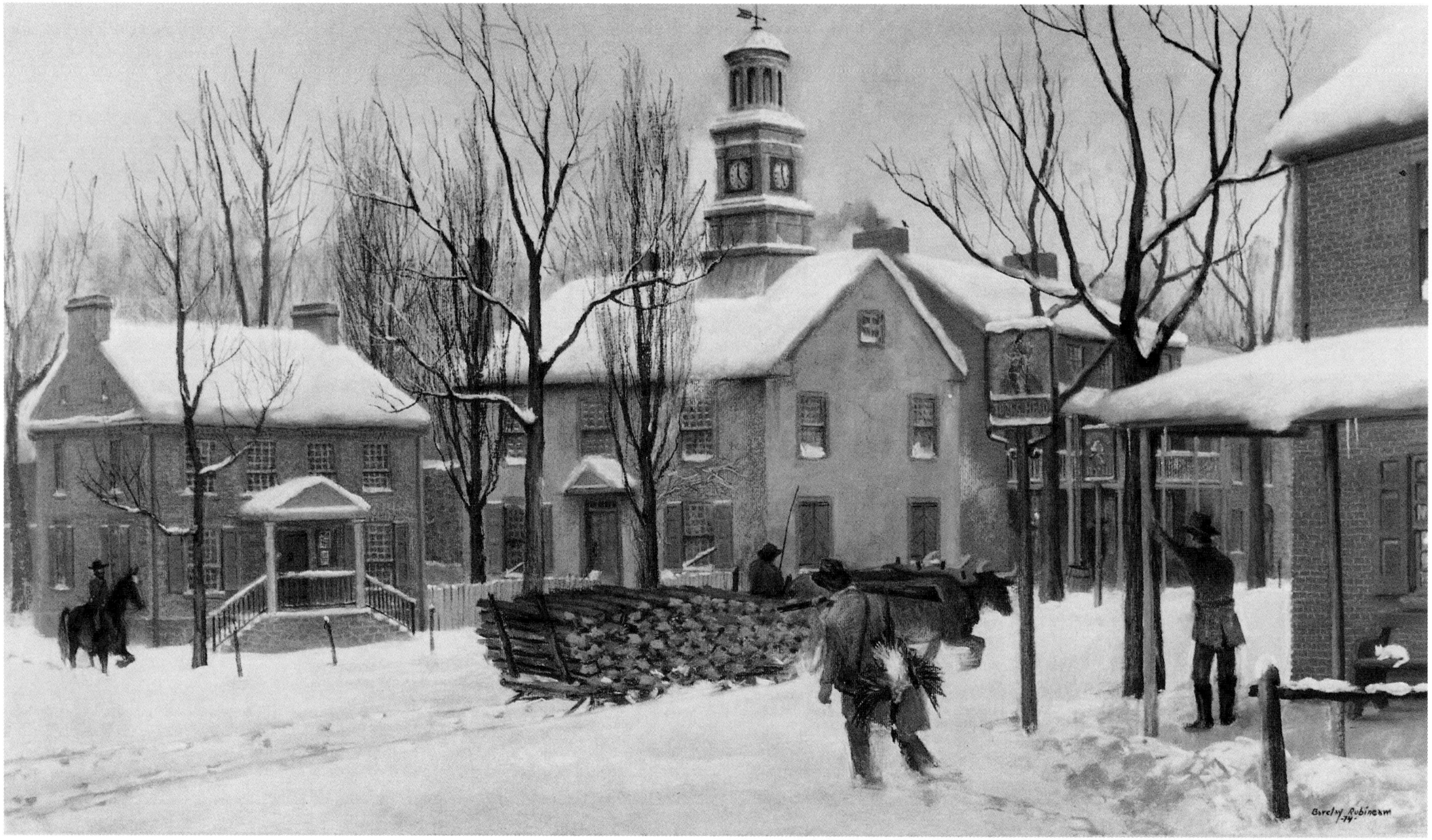

11. "Turk's Head"
(West Side, High and
Market St.)

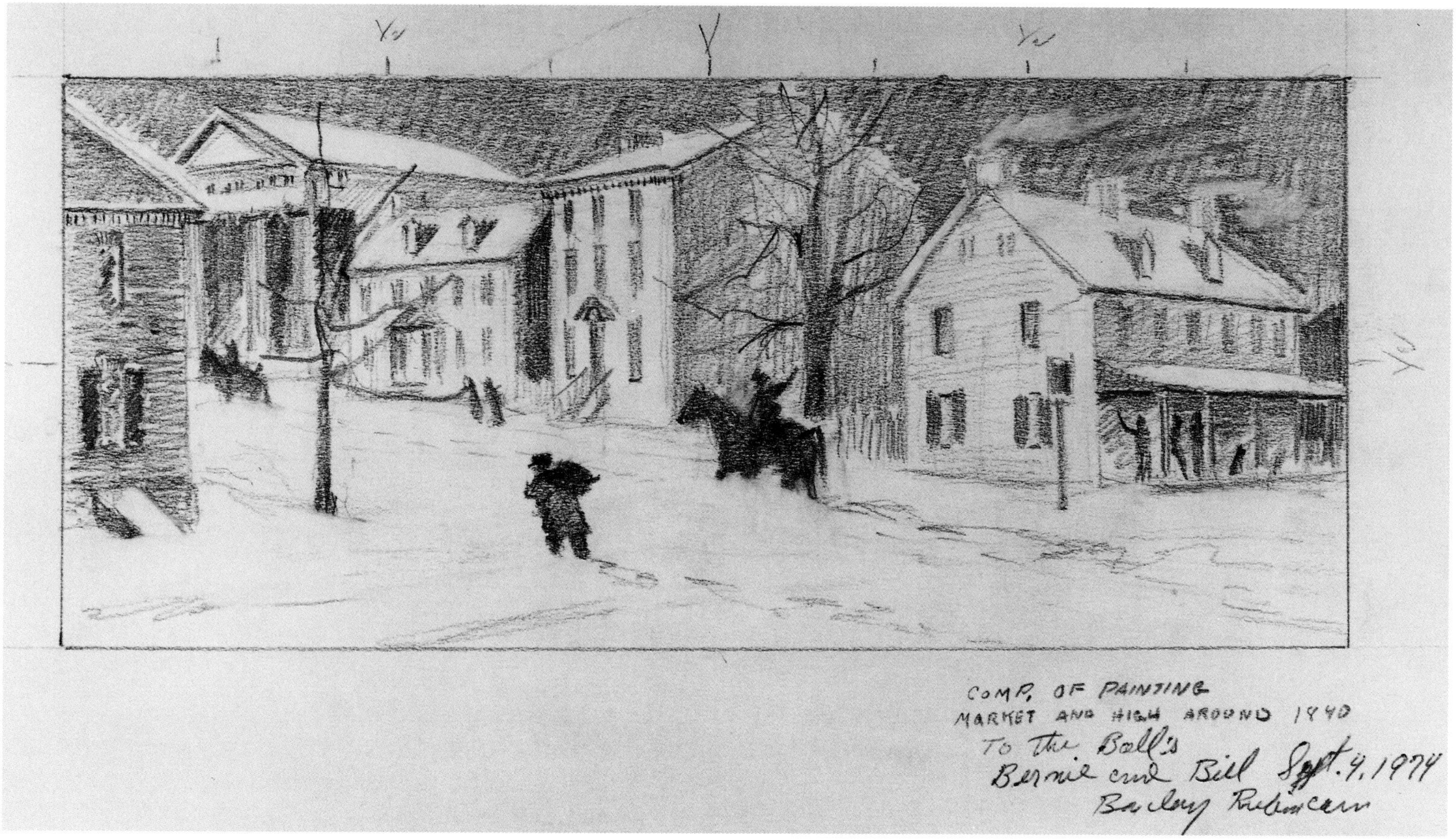

12. Sketch for "Turk's Head"

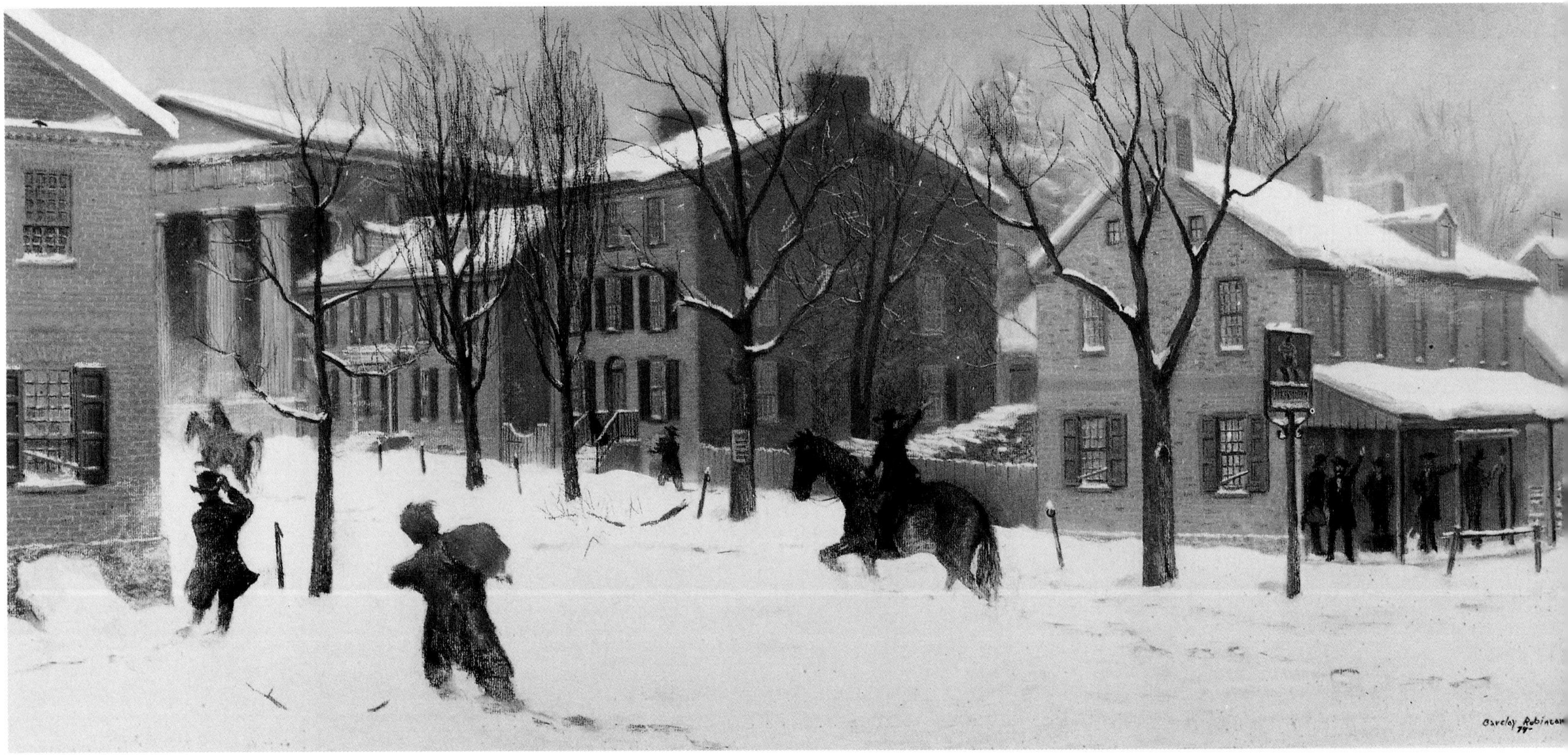

13. "Turk's Head"
(East Side, High and
Market St.)

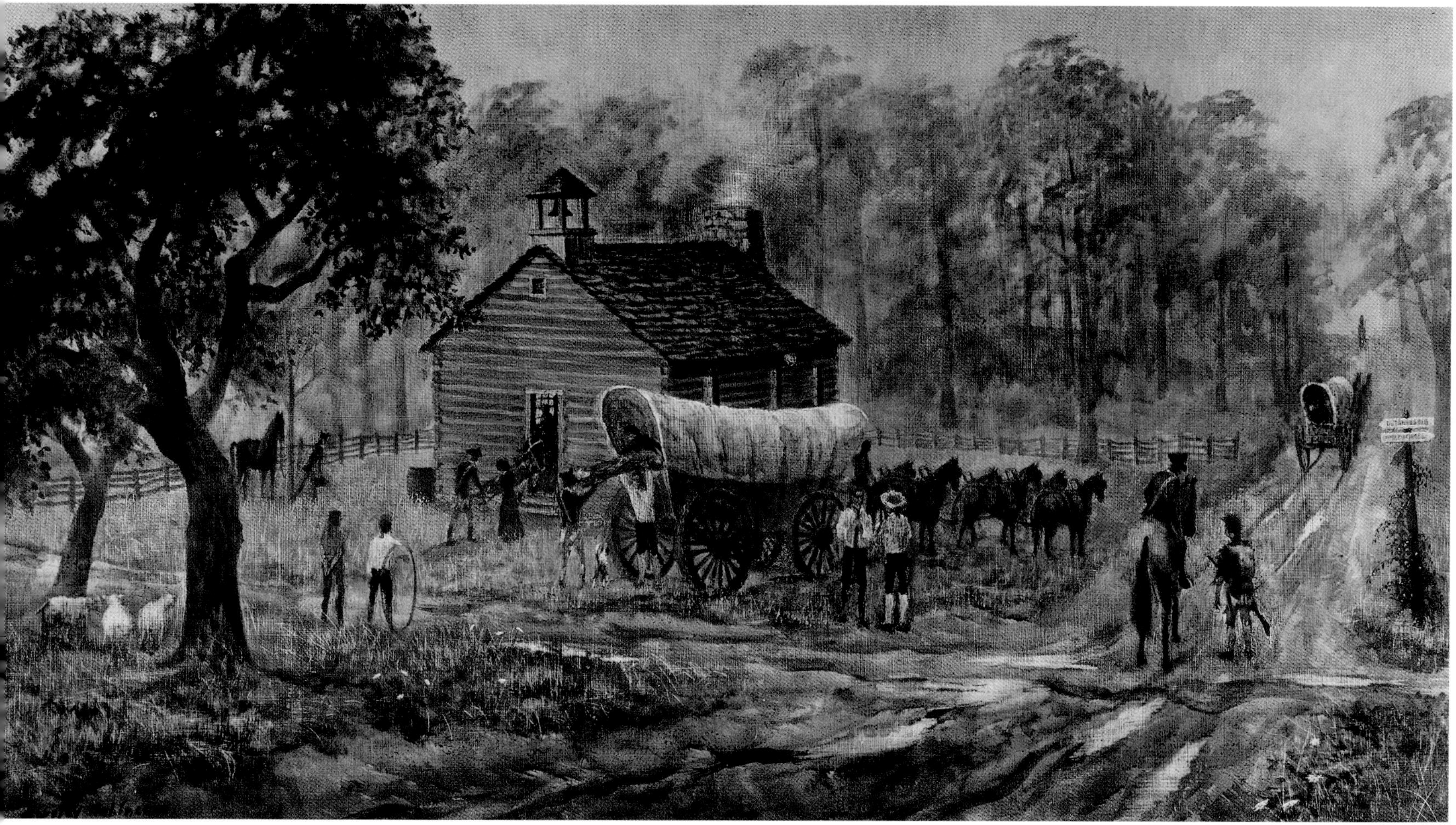

14. Turk's Head Log Schoolhouse

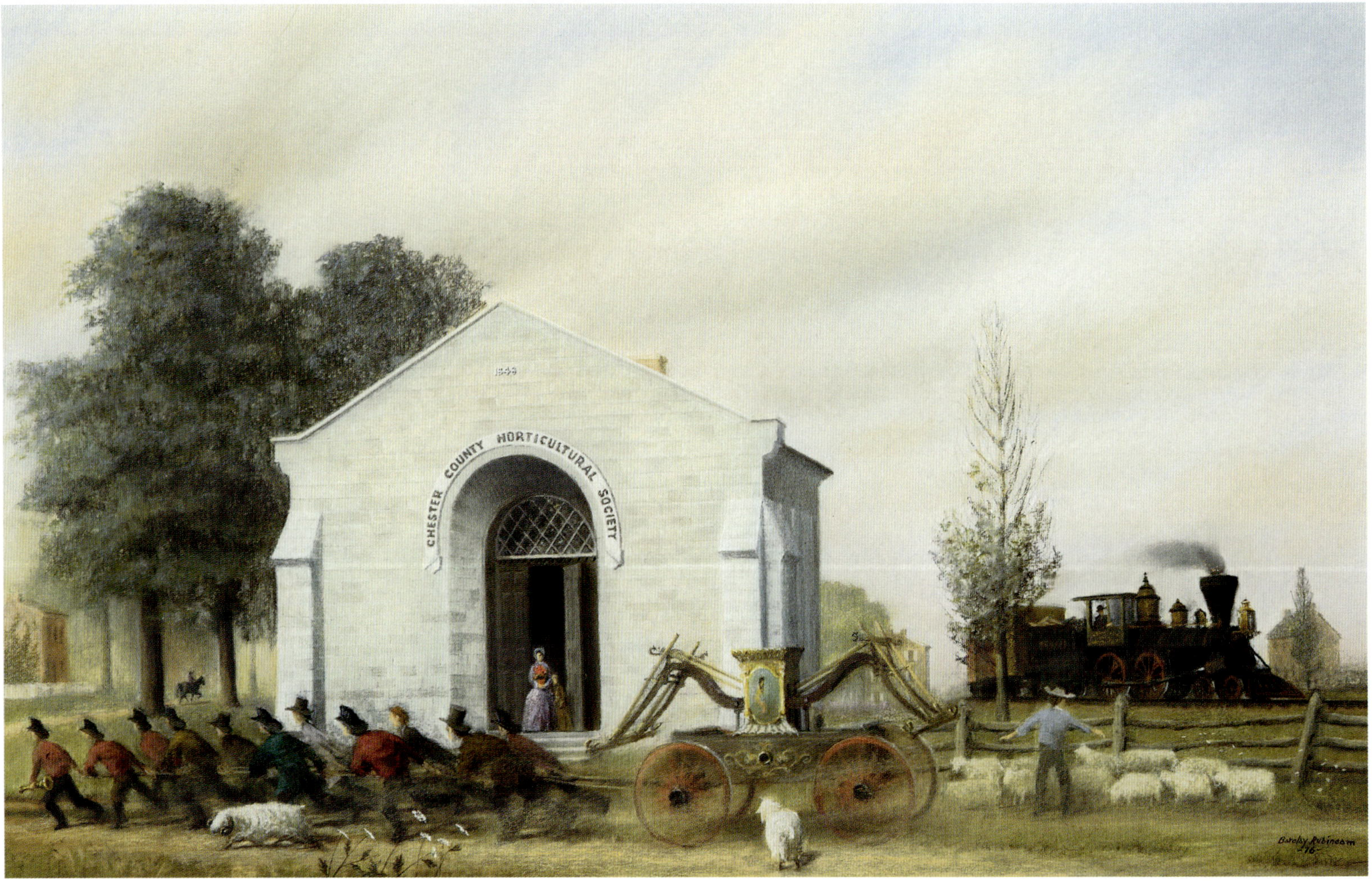

15. Old Horticultural Hall

The History Paintings

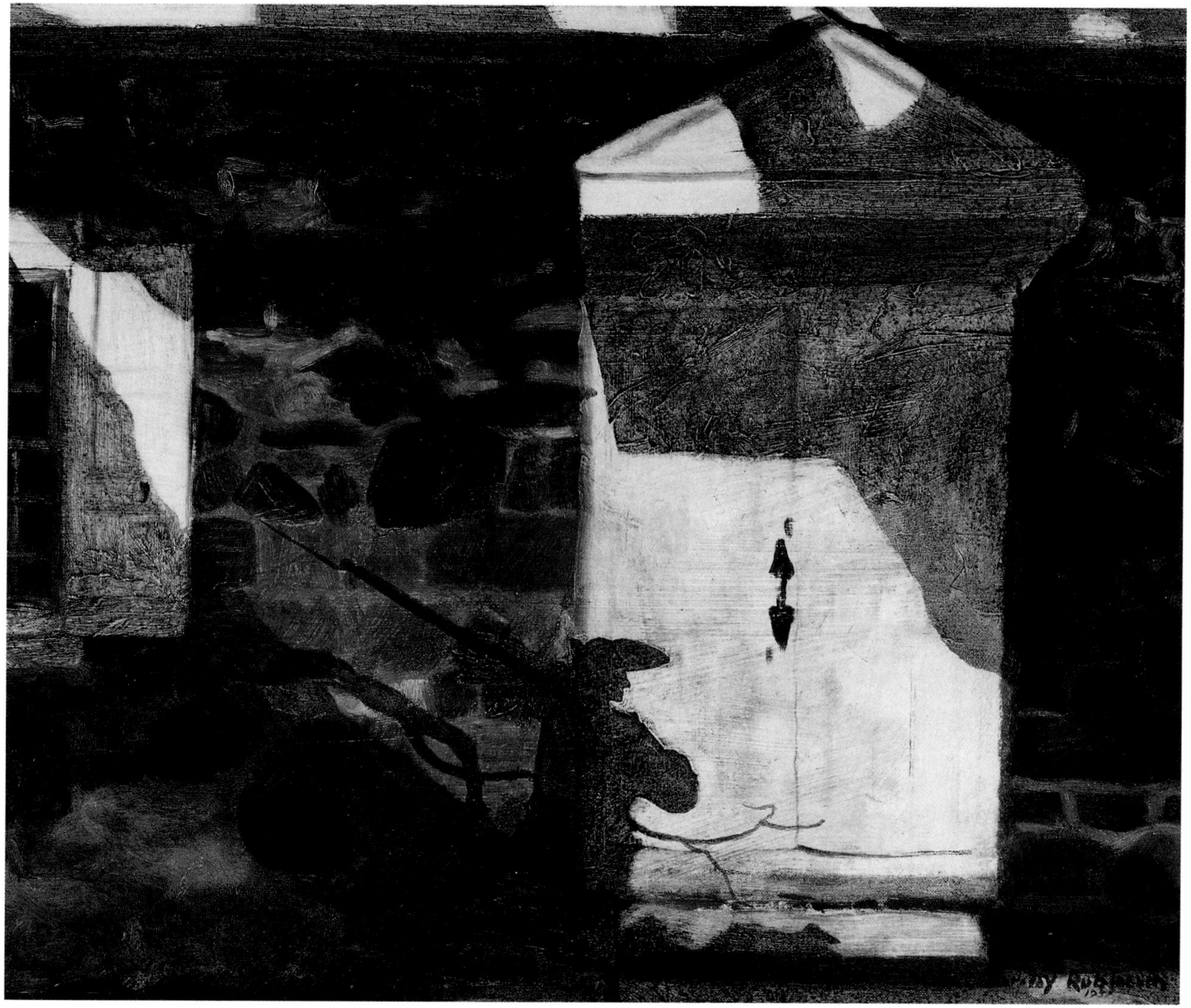

The battle of British and American troops during the American Revolution haunts many Rubincam paintings. The two armies clashed in Chester County at the Battle of Brandywine on September 11, 1777. This dramatic encounter and the events leading up to it reappear frequently in Rubincam's work. Some tell the narrative directly, others depict ghostlike shadows of the period. In a change of topic, the artist also revealed his grasp of Civil War history in his portrayal of the Battle of Gettysburg.

16. Study for Sentry at Birmingham

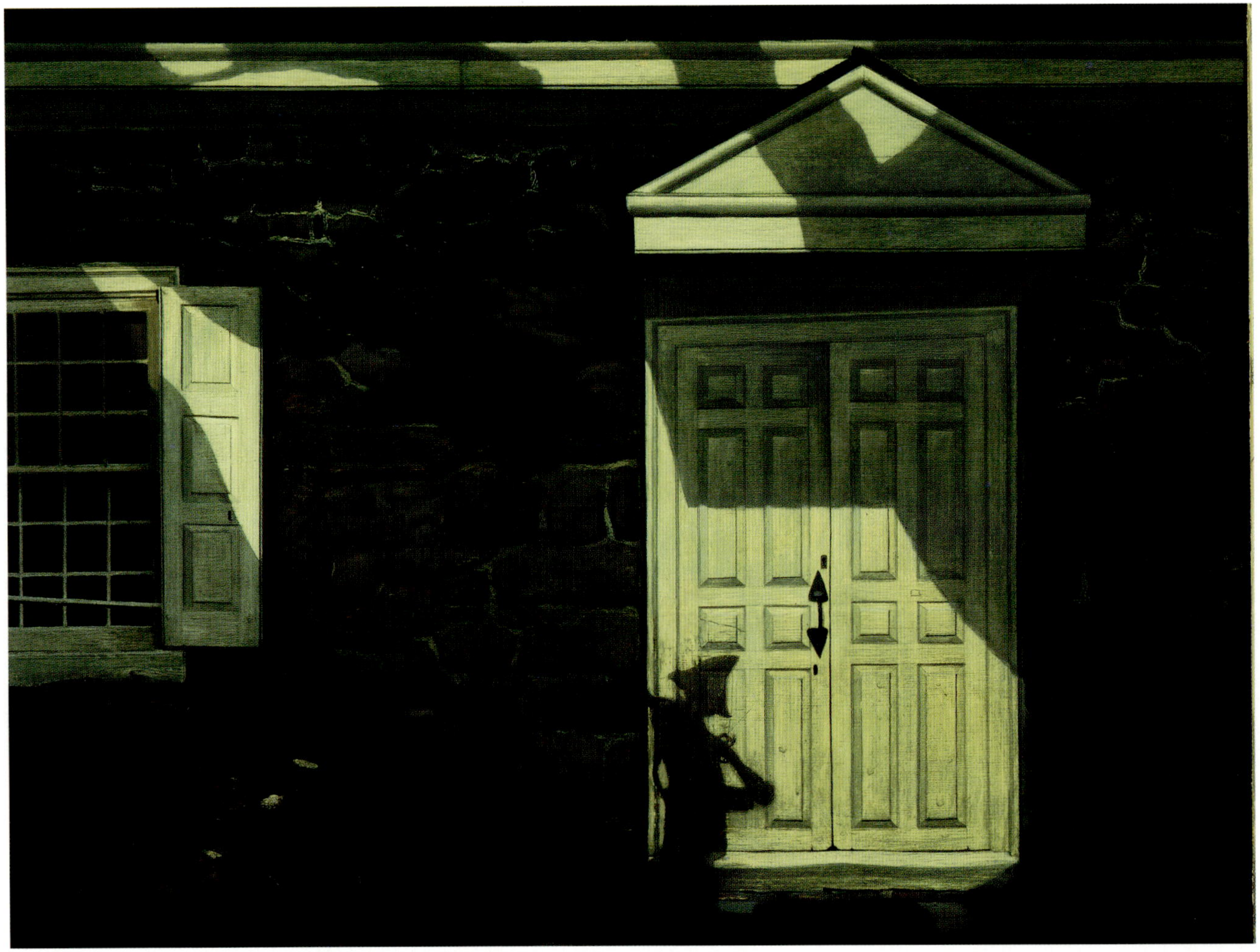

17. Sentry at Birmingham

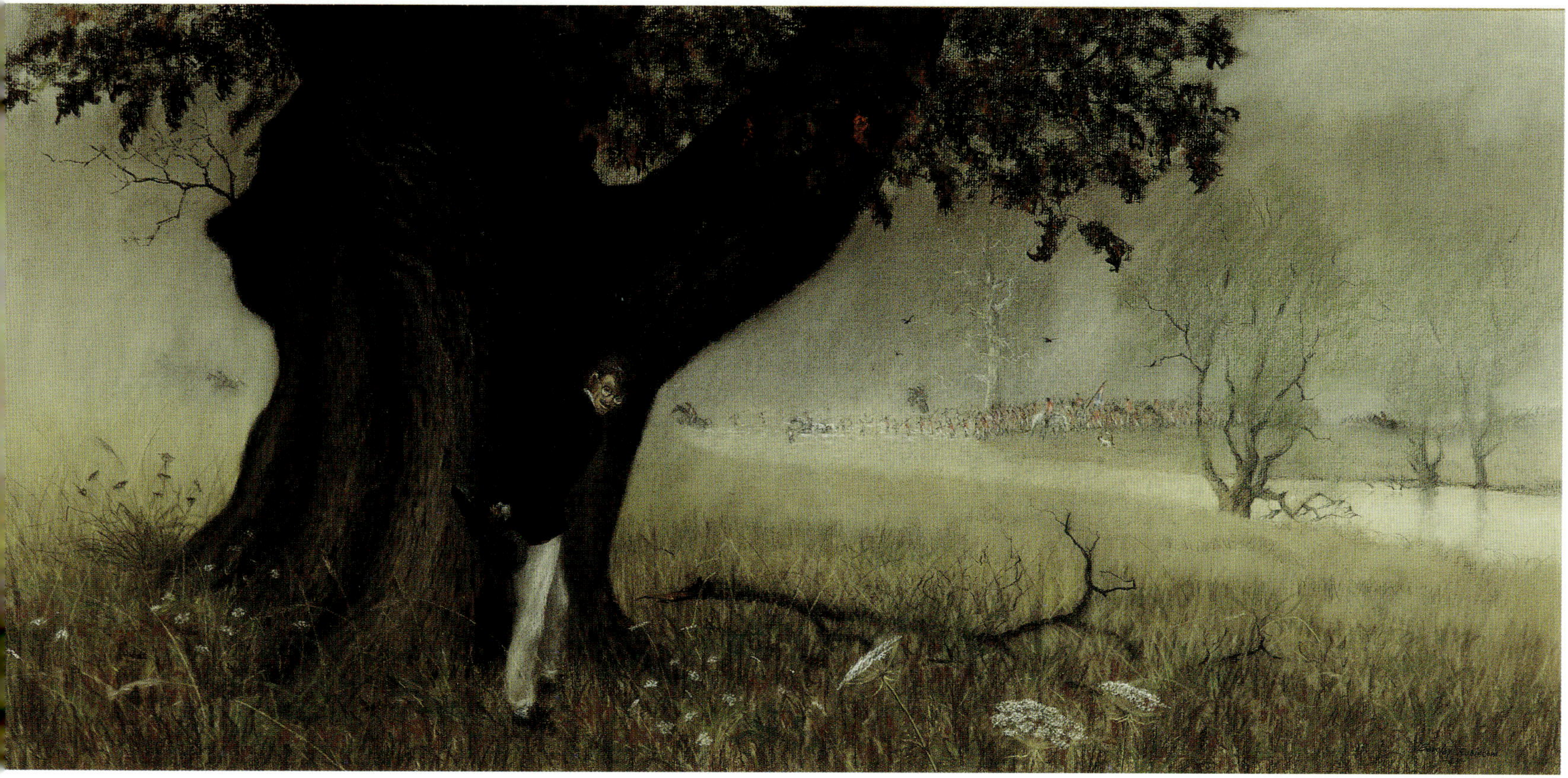

18. Jefferis Ford, Sept. 11, 1777

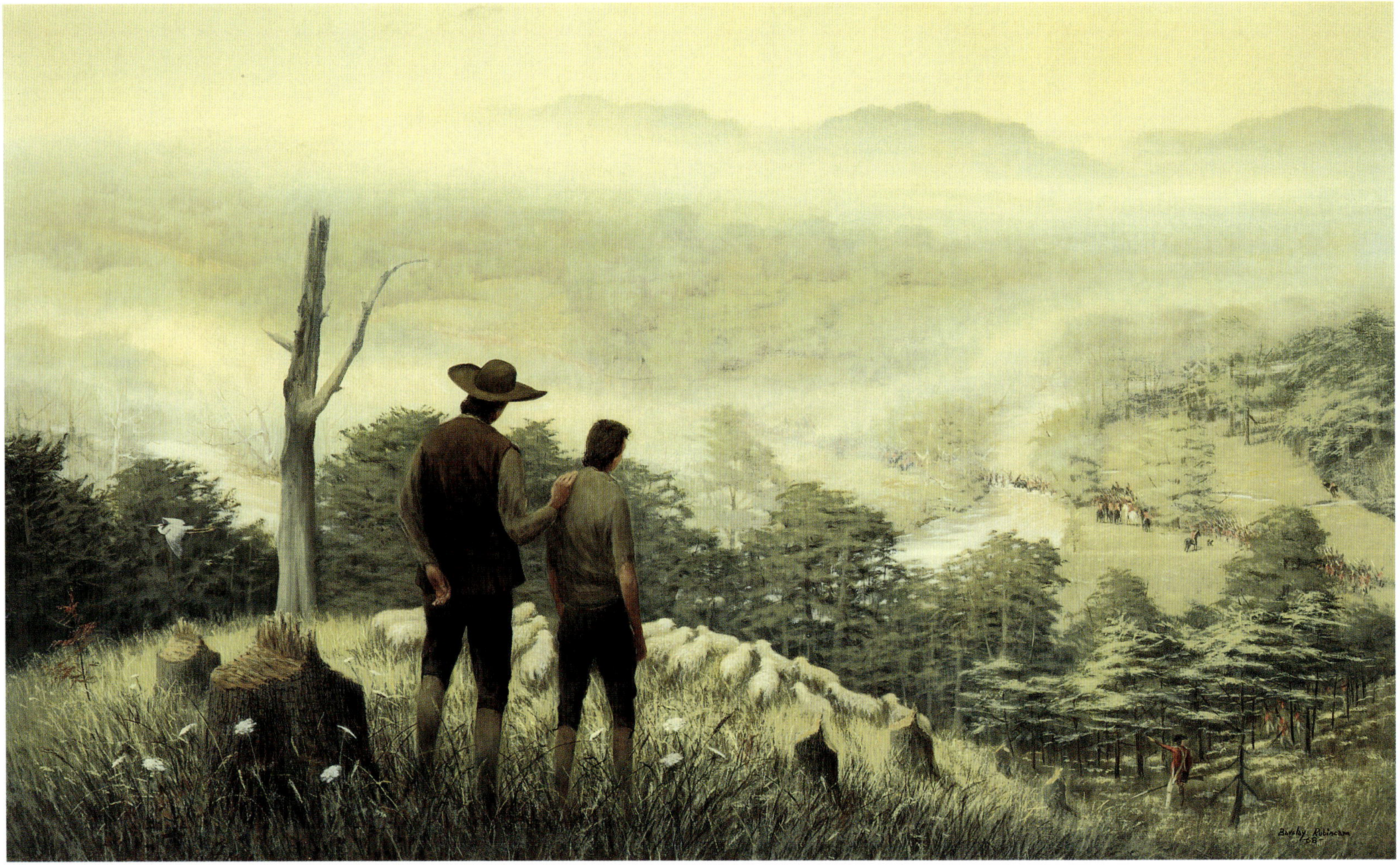

19. The Trap Was Sprung

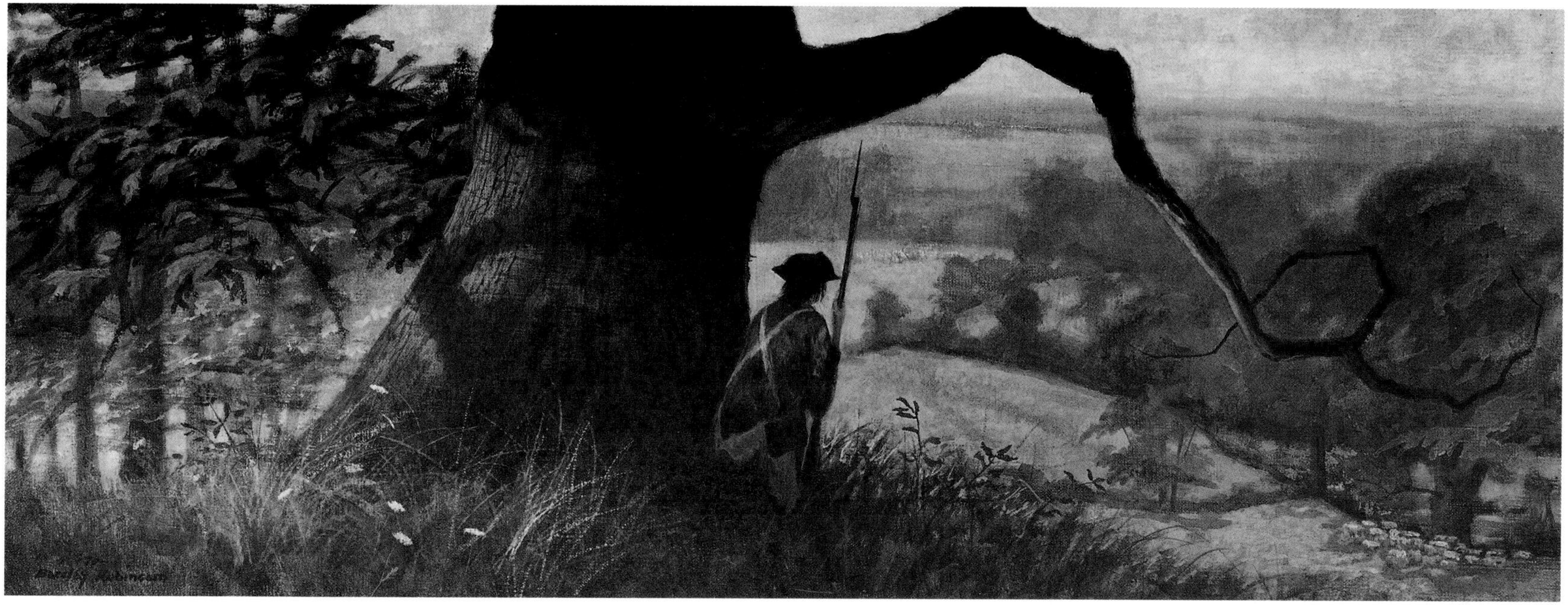

20. Revolutionary Soldier

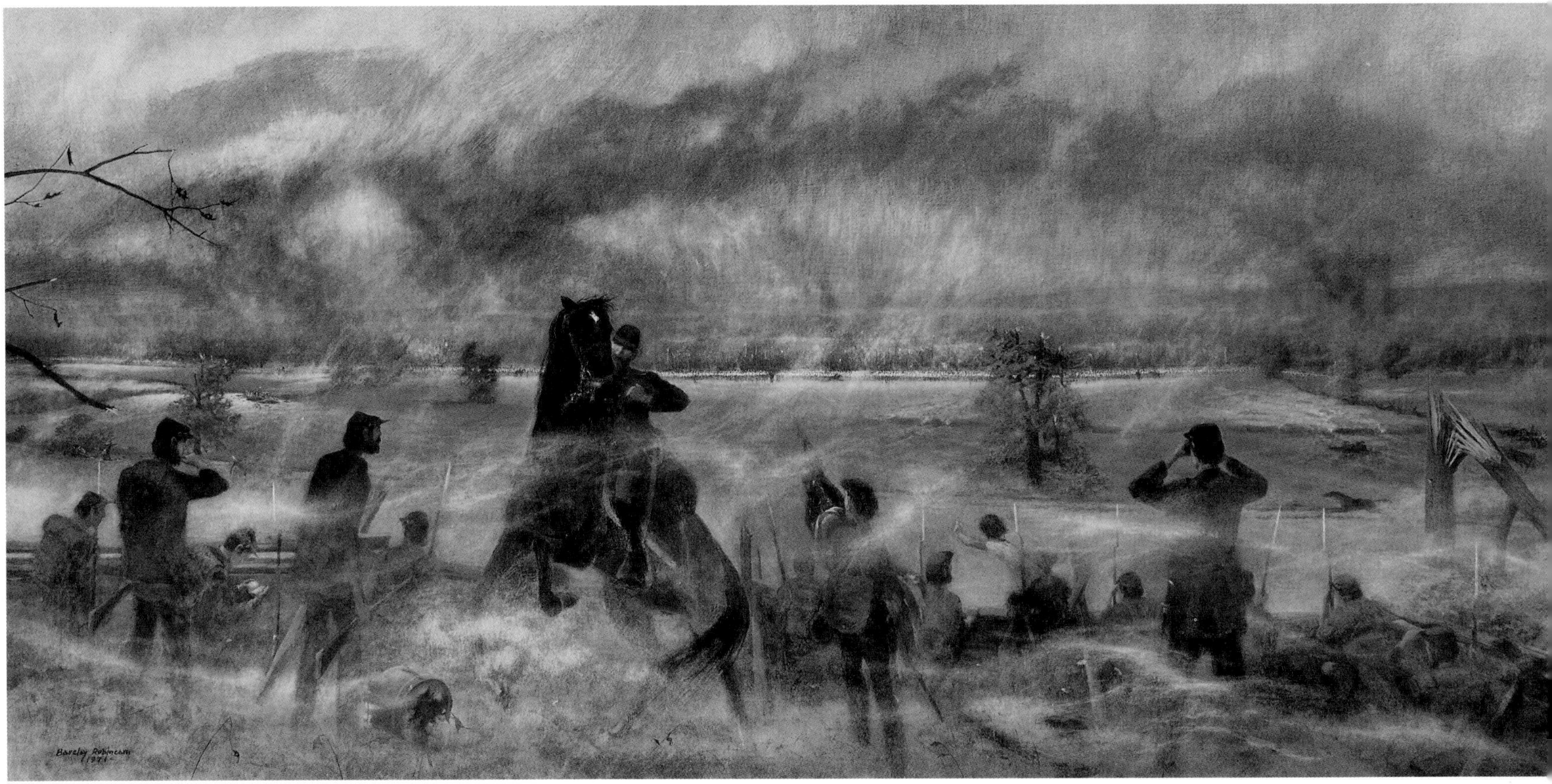

21. Gettysburg, around
3 p.m., July 3, 1863

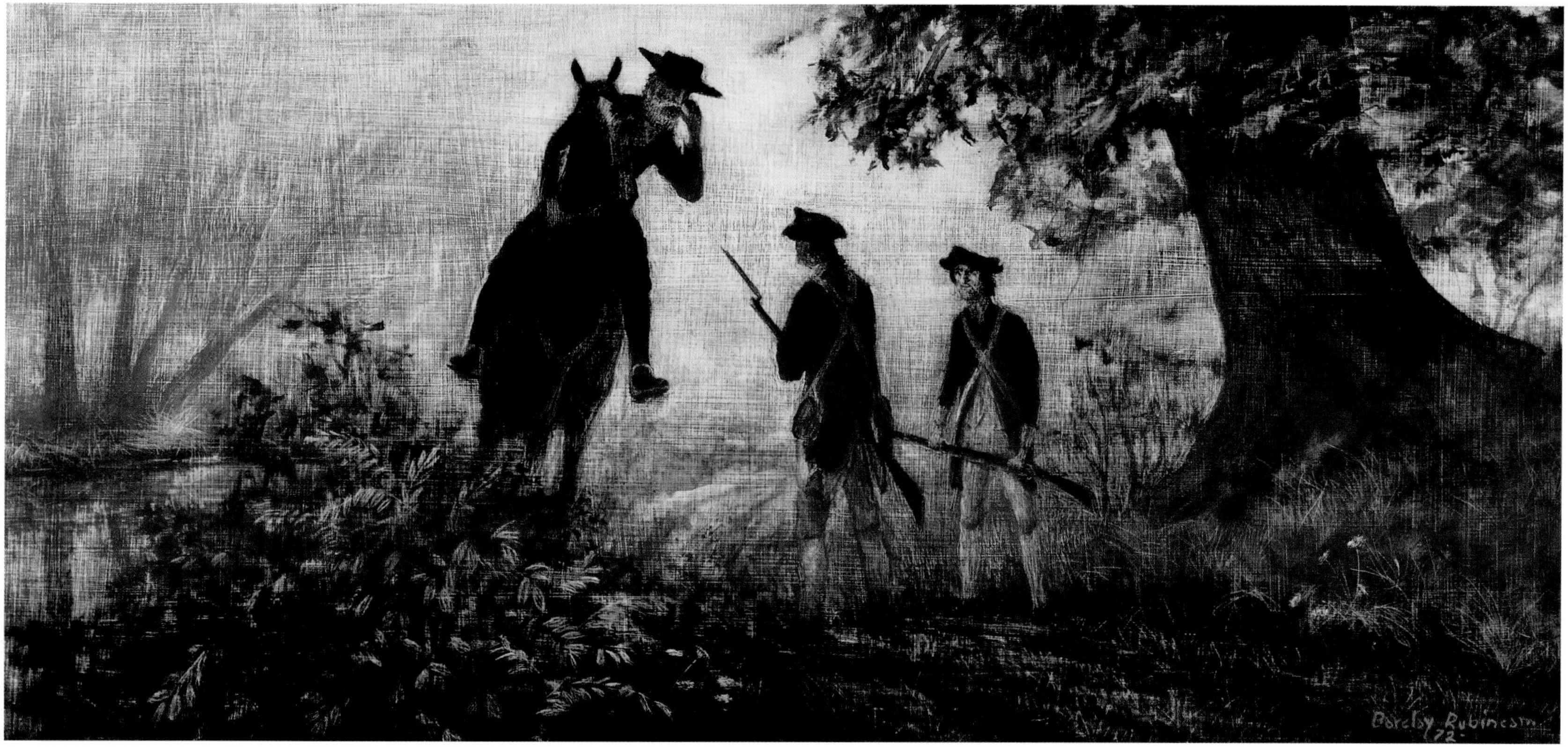

22. Squire Cheney "Chester County Patriot"

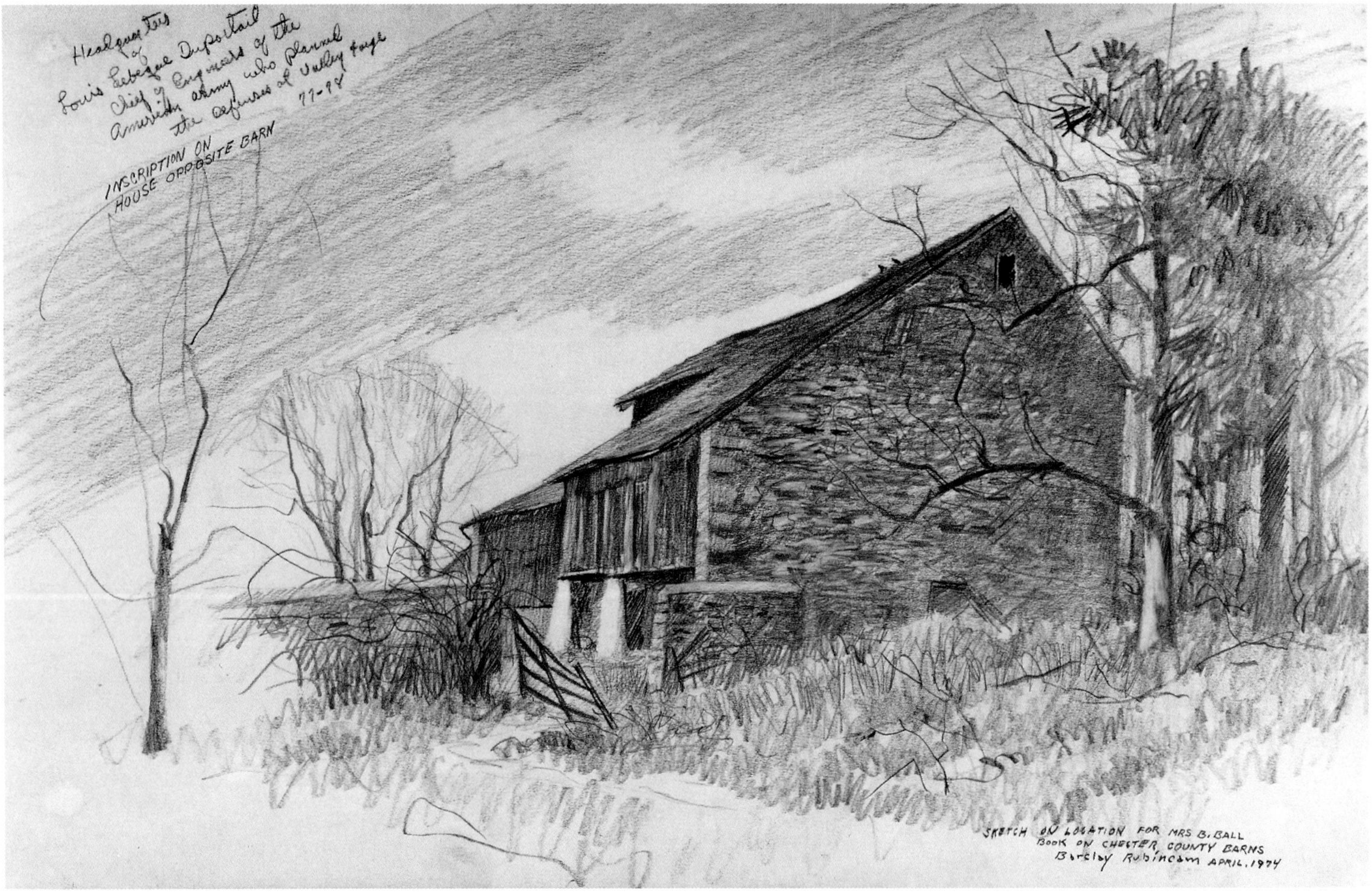

23. Sketch for A
Chesterbrook Barn

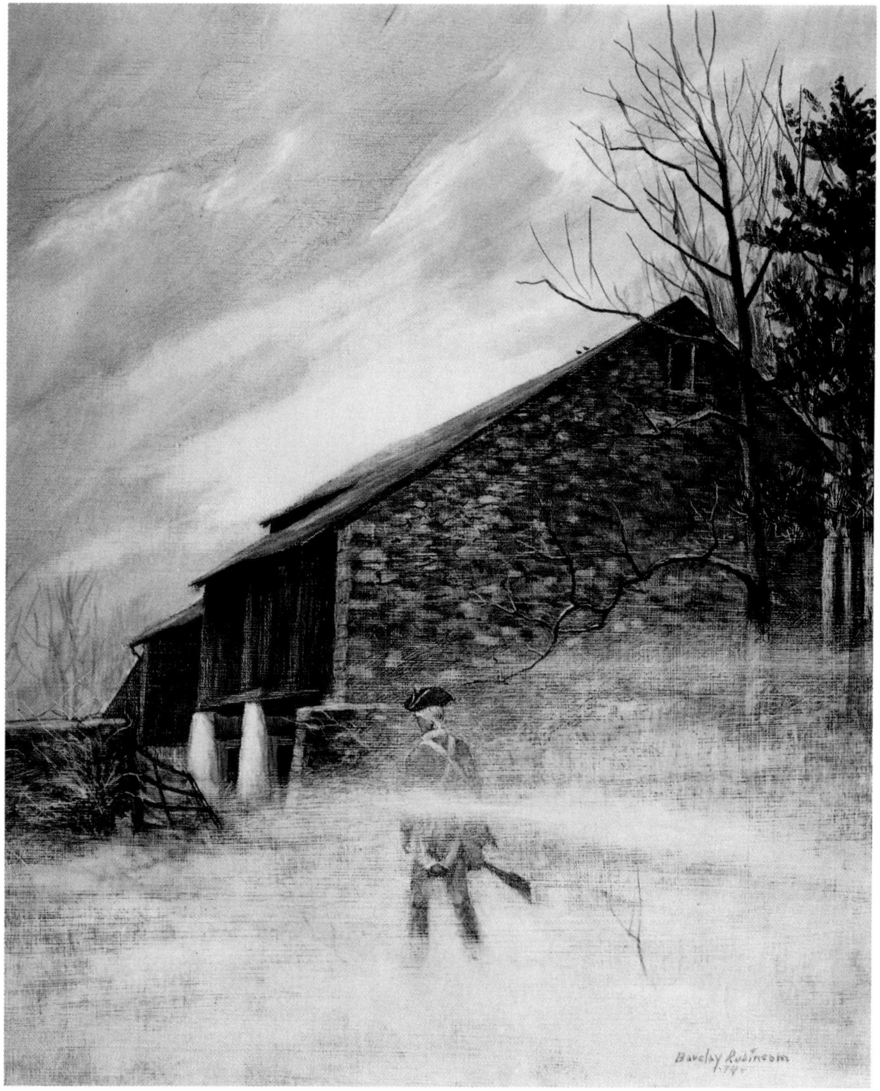

24. A Chesterbrook Barn

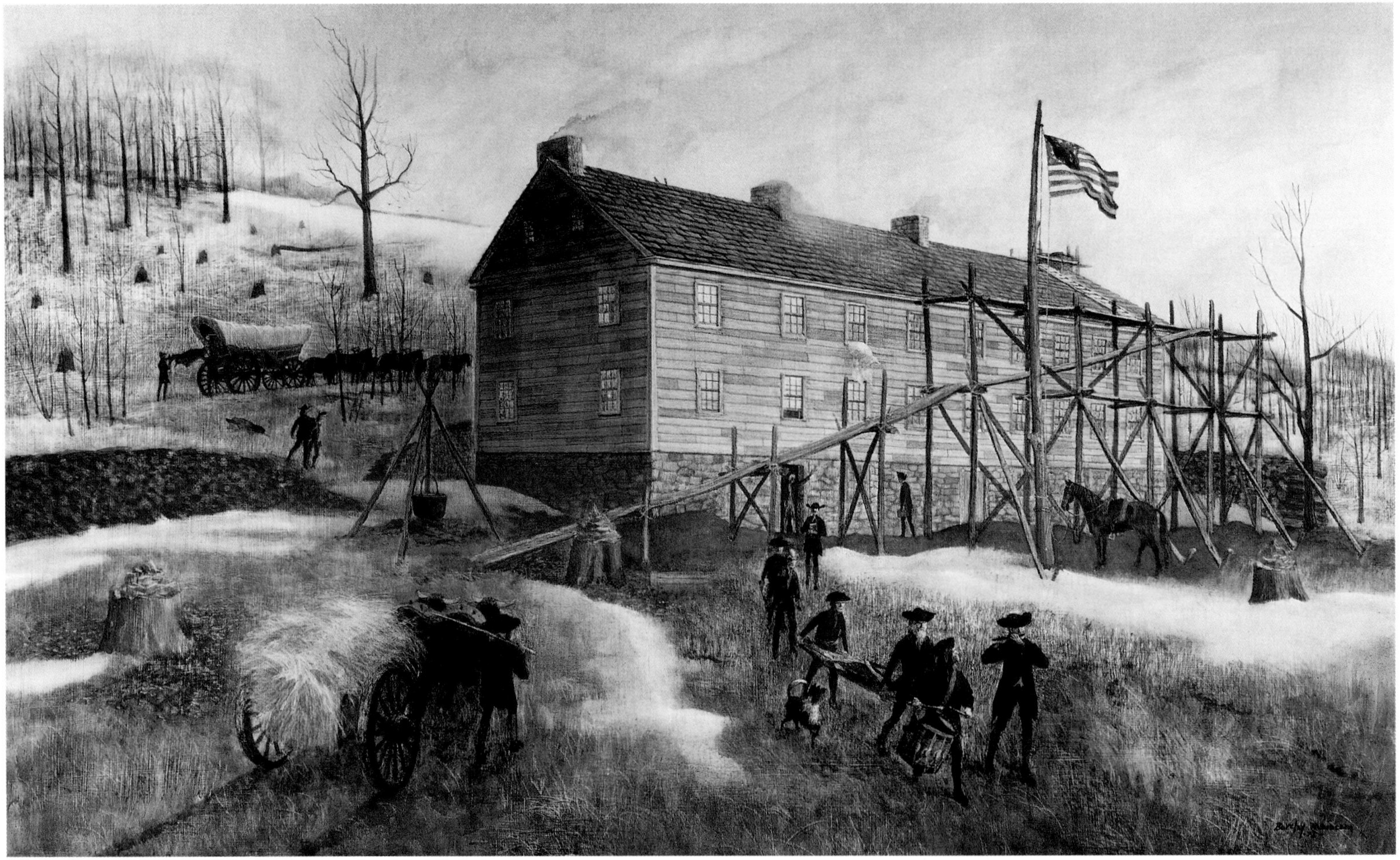

25. The Revolutionary War Hospital at Yellow Springs

Landscapes

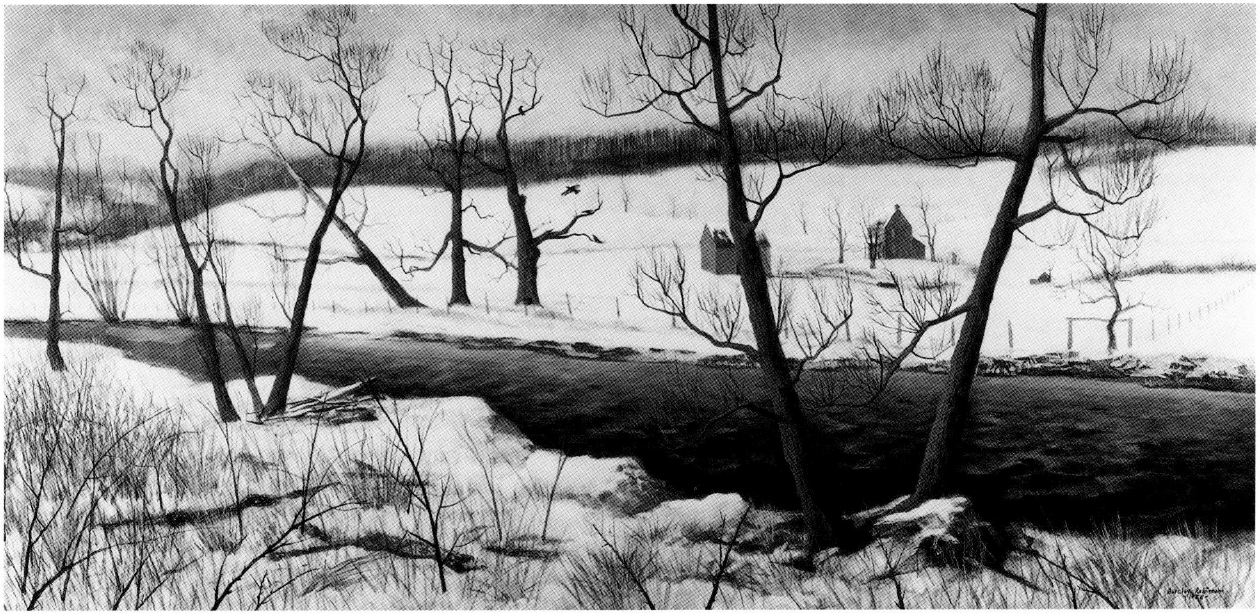

26. Brandywine, East Branch

For Barclay Rubincam, the landscapes of Chester County offered endless inspiration. His paintings reveal an outdoorsman's sensitivity to the varied forms of hillsides, fields and meandering streams. With a subtle touch, he captured seasonal changes, morning and evening light, rising mist and falling snow. The artist never tired of the land he knew so well, rediscovering its beauty within each familiar view.

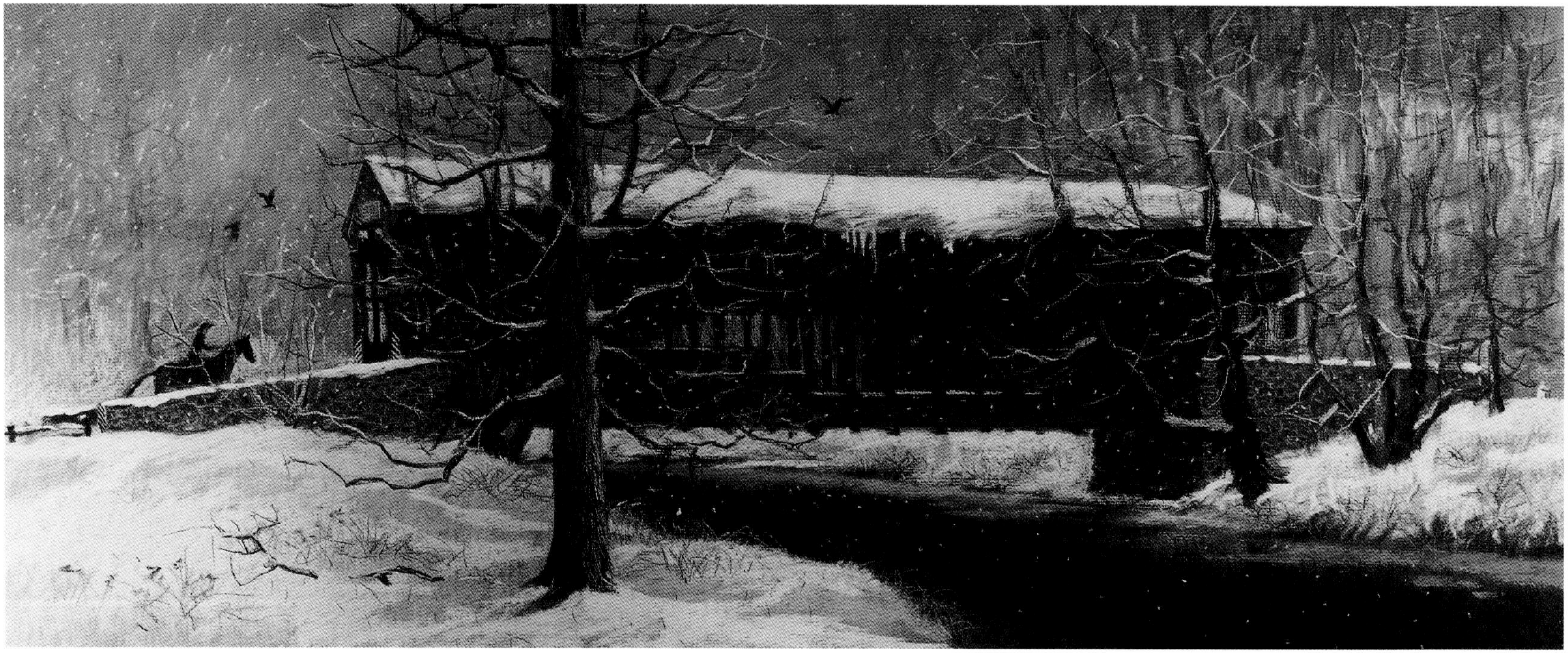

27. Shaw's Bridge

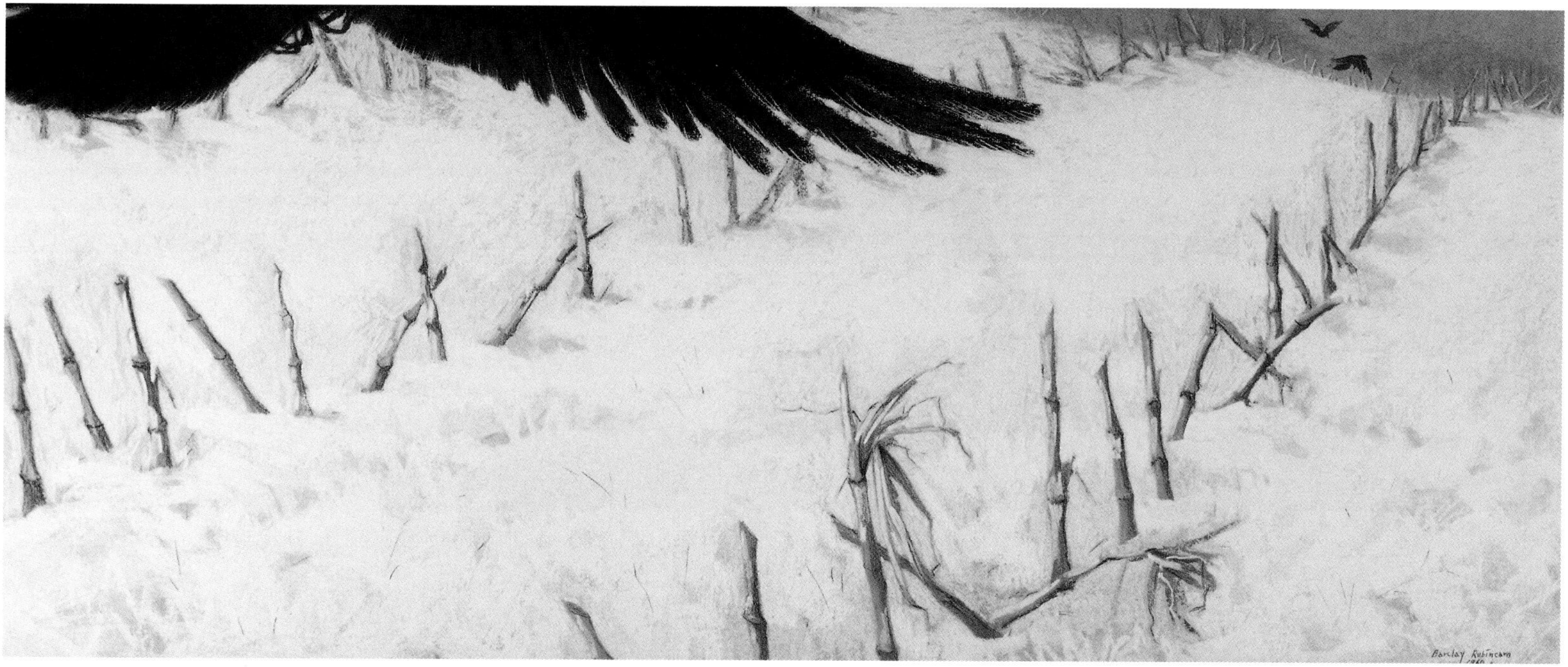

28. The Corn Field

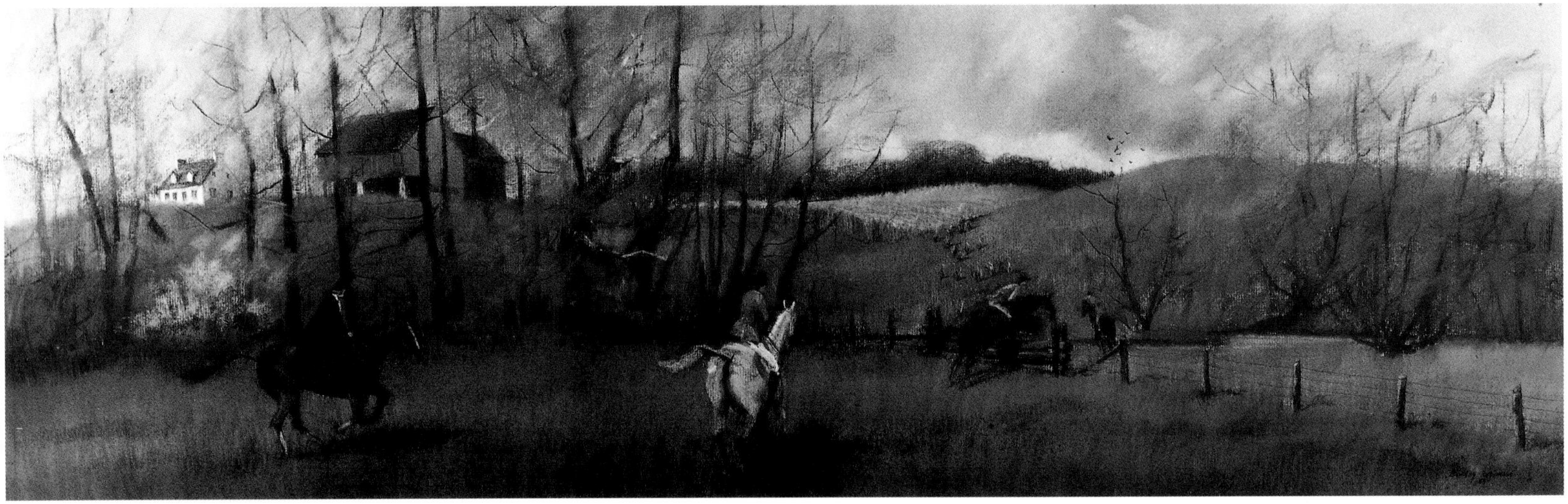

29. In Full Cry

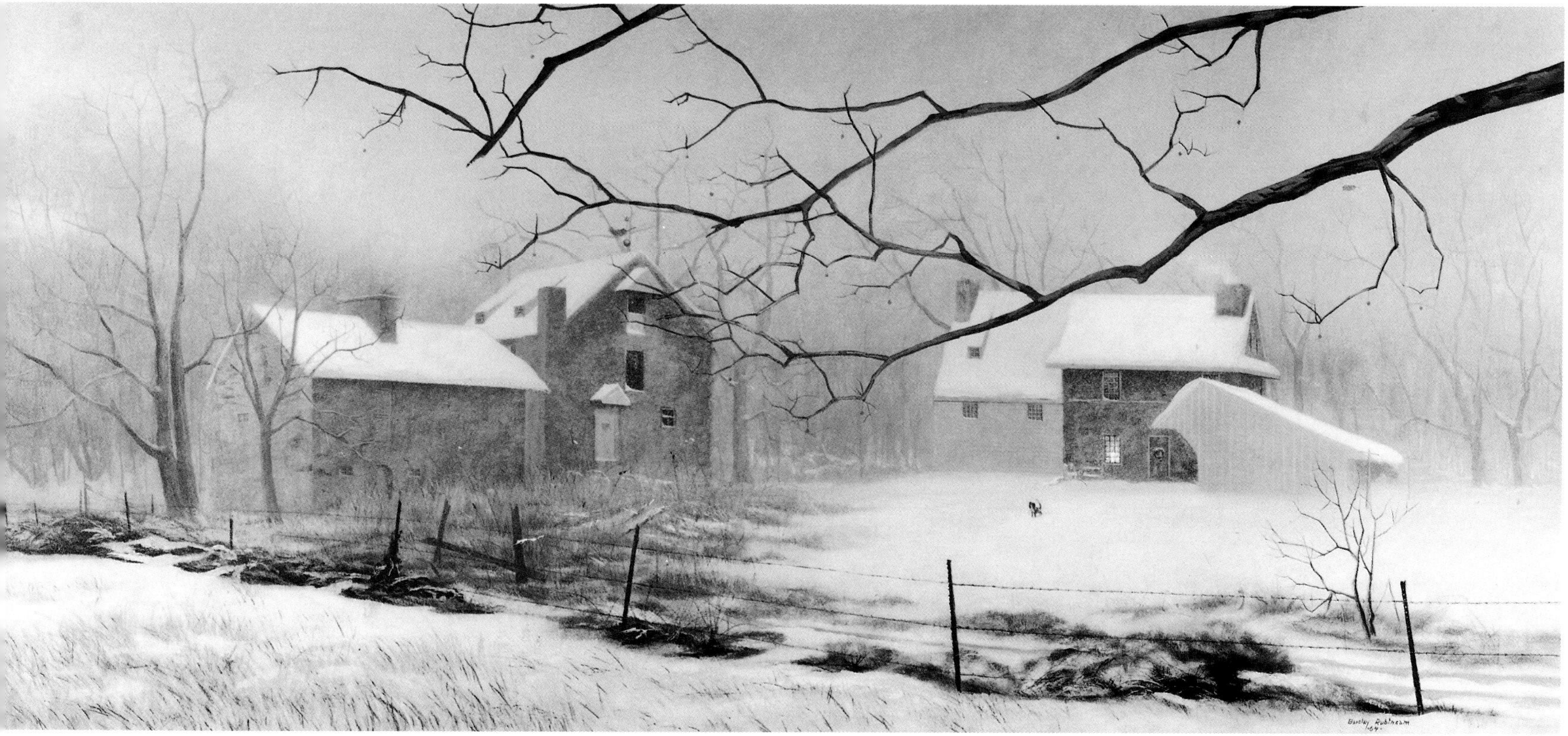

30. Andrew Wyeth's Mill

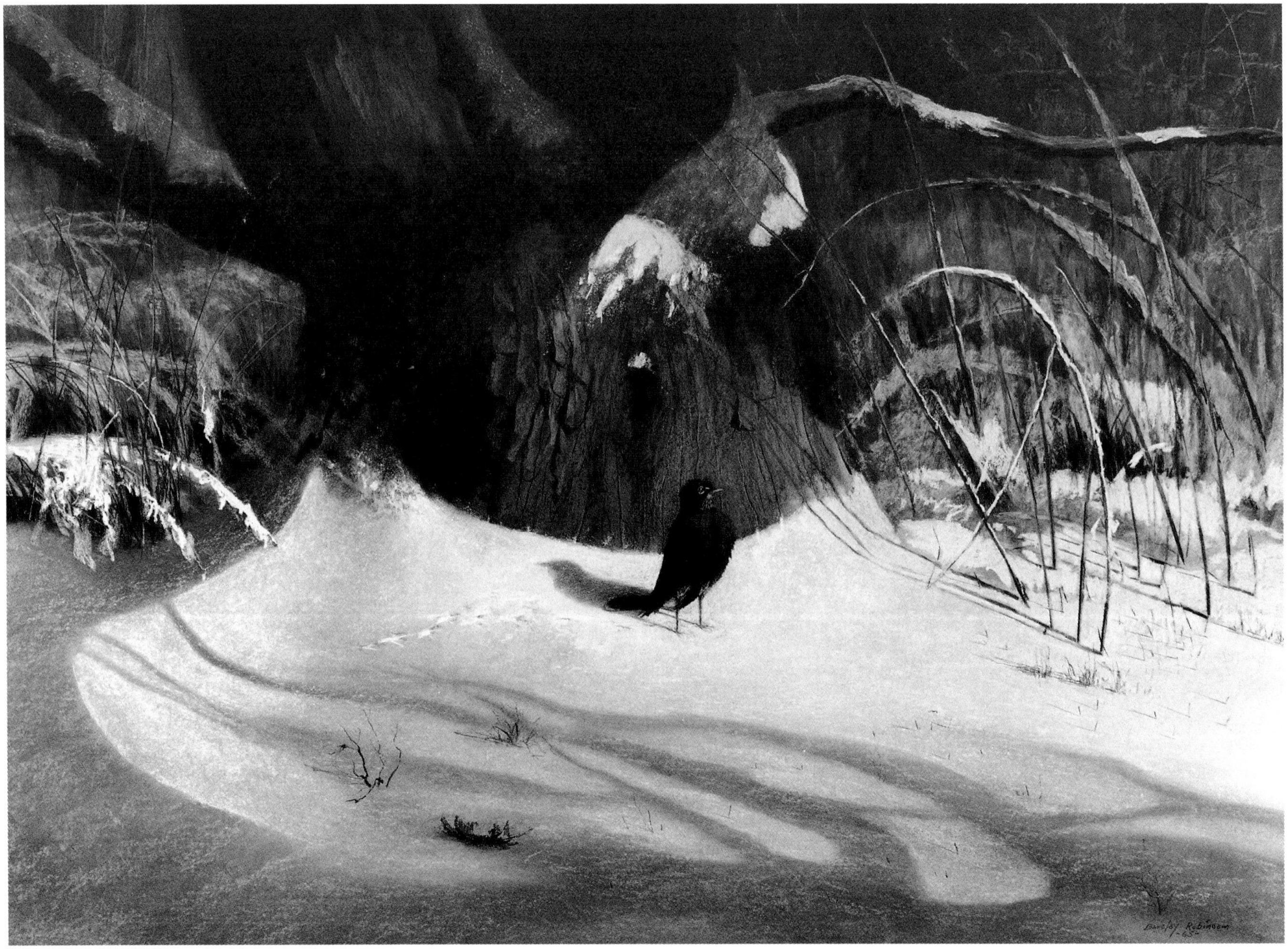

31. Spring Snow

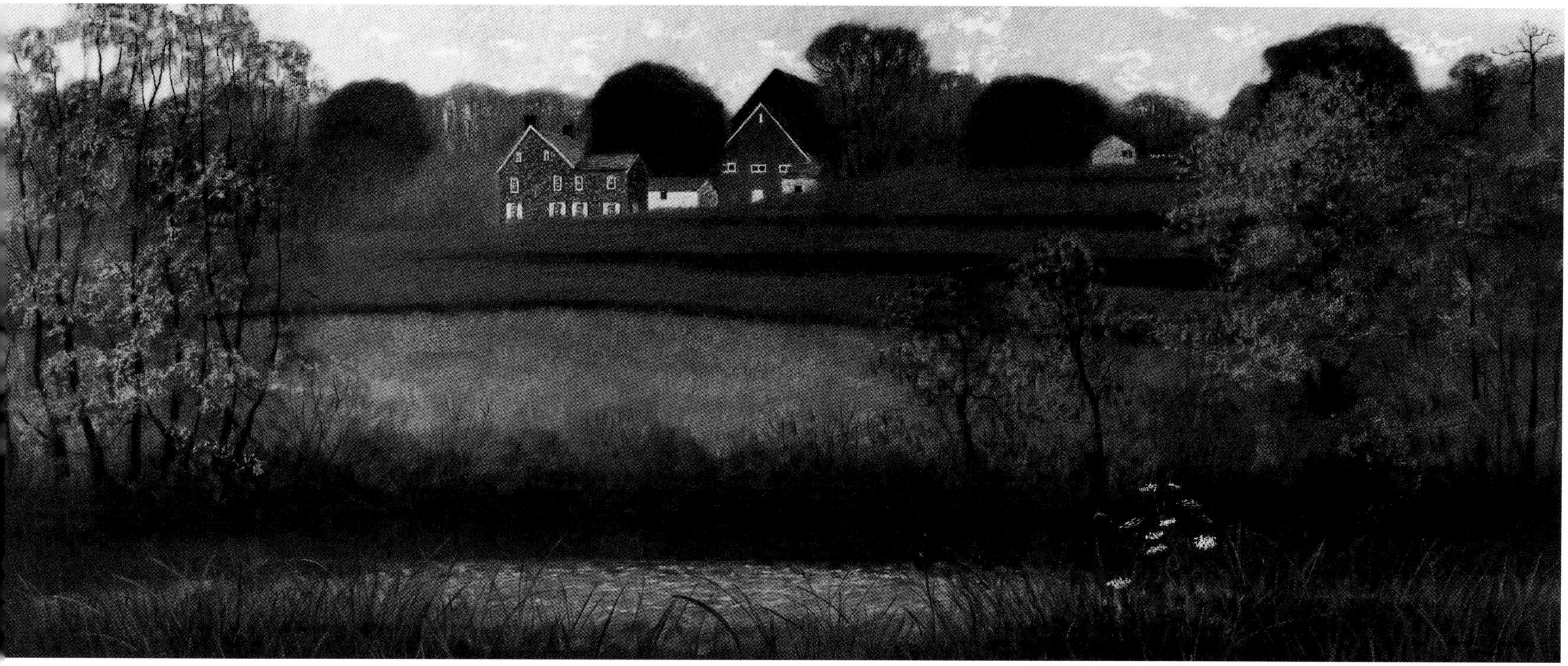

32. "After the Rain"

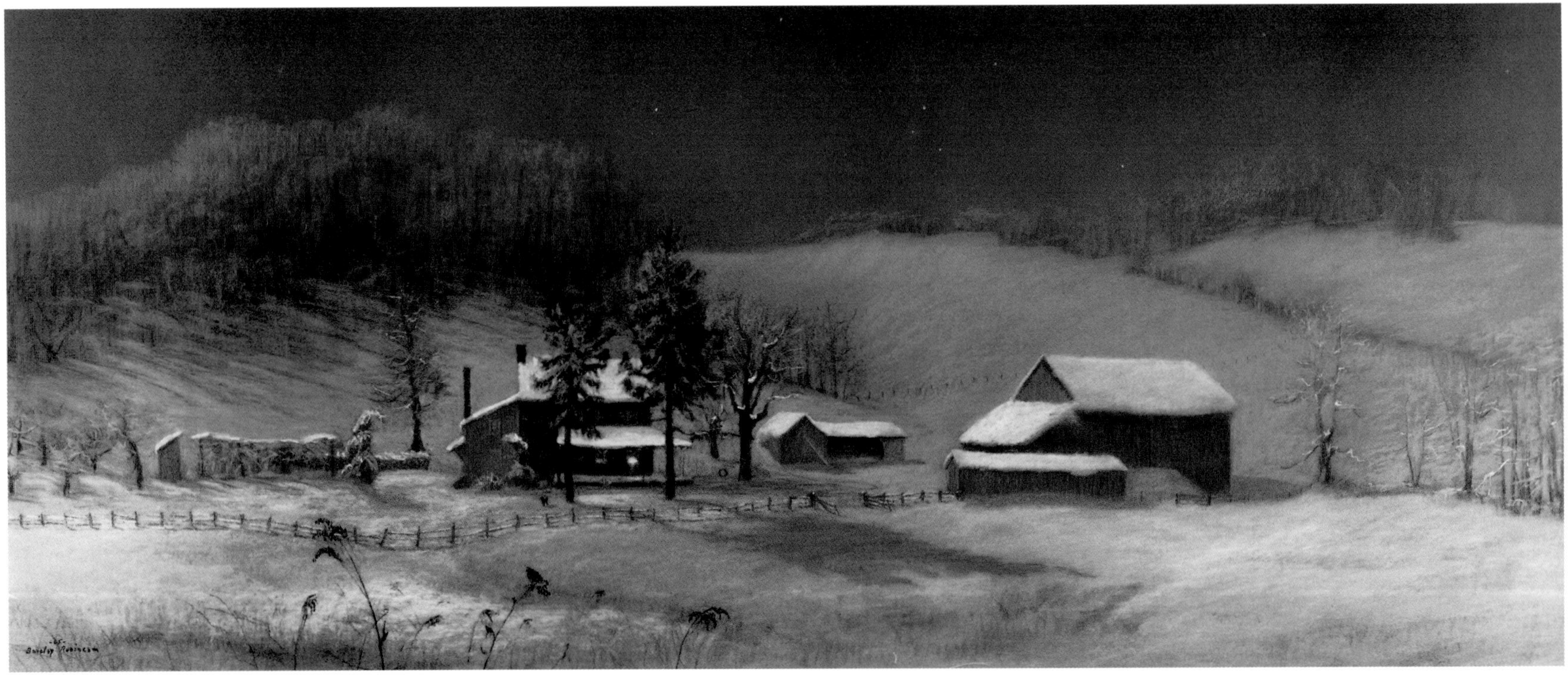

33. Farmhouse on Winter Night

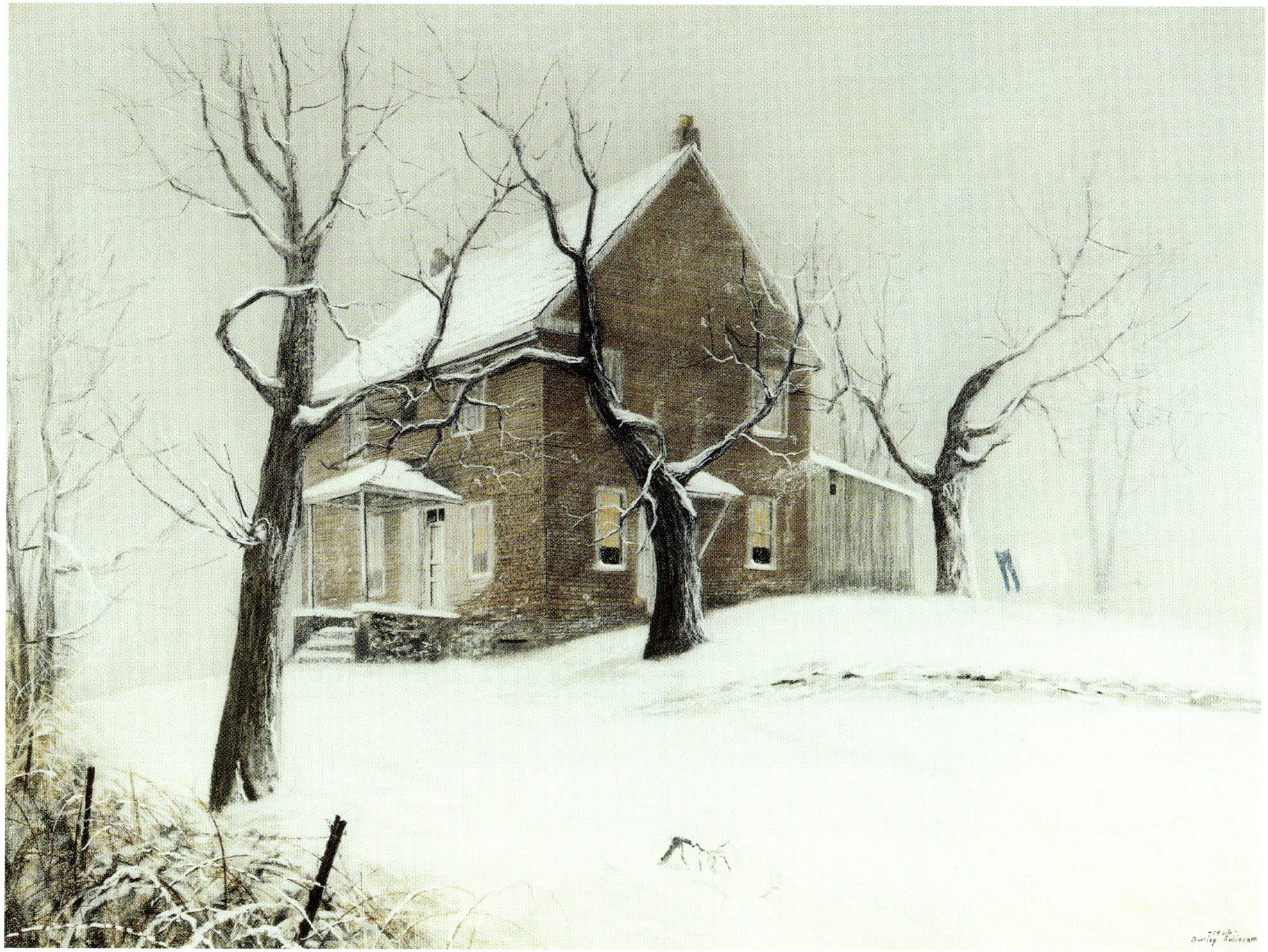

34. 1724 House built by
Abiah Taylor

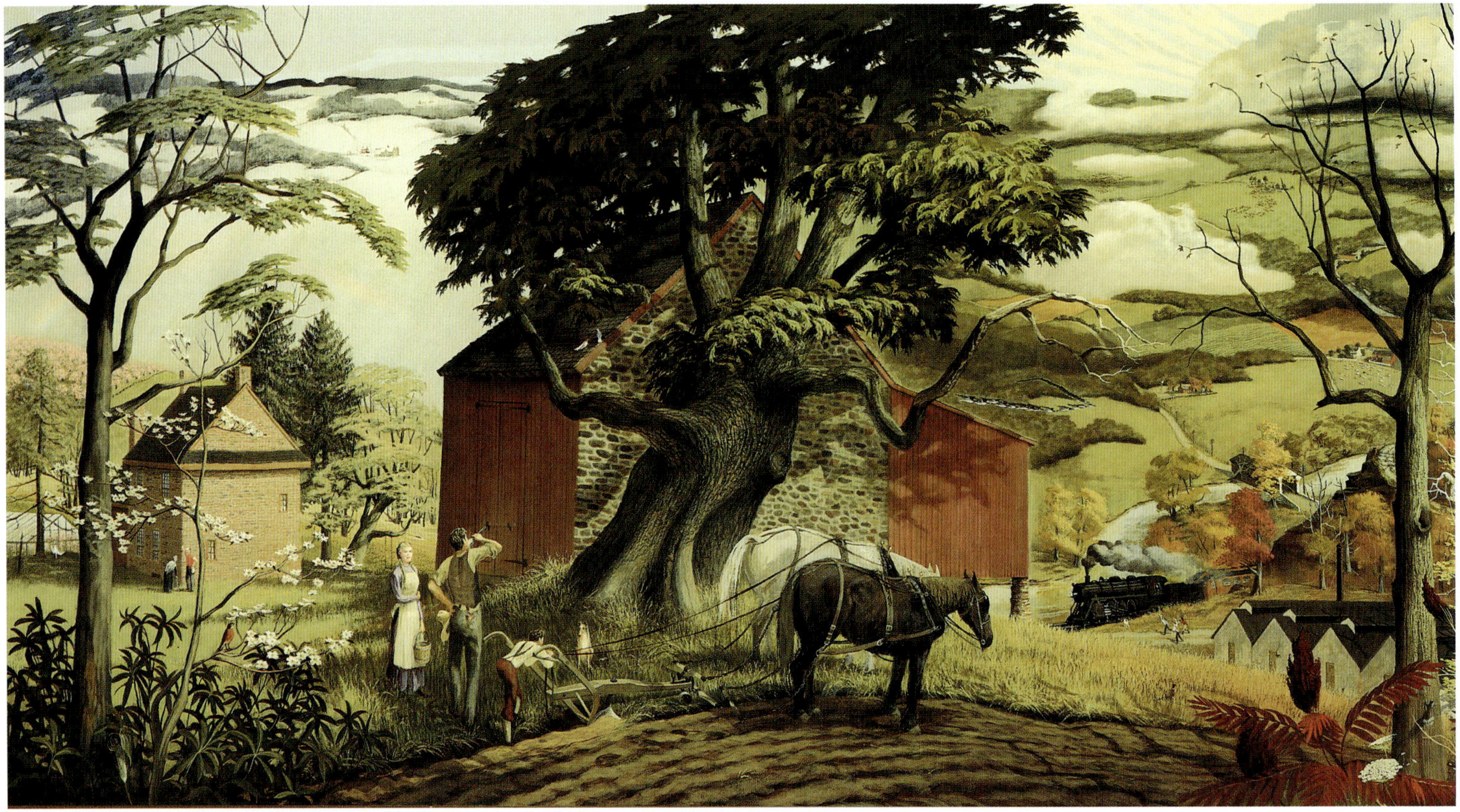

35. The Four Seasons

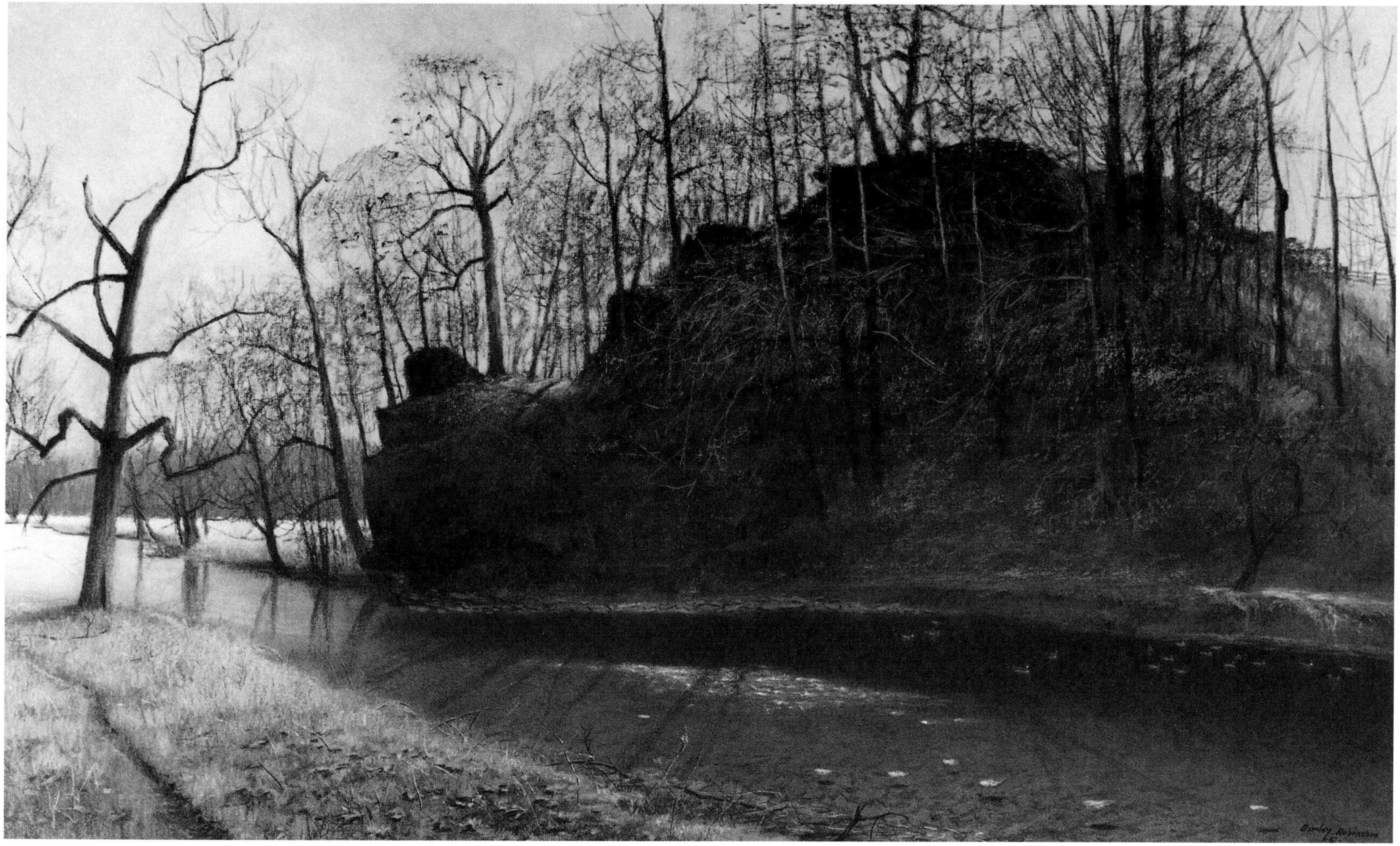

36. Deborah's Rock

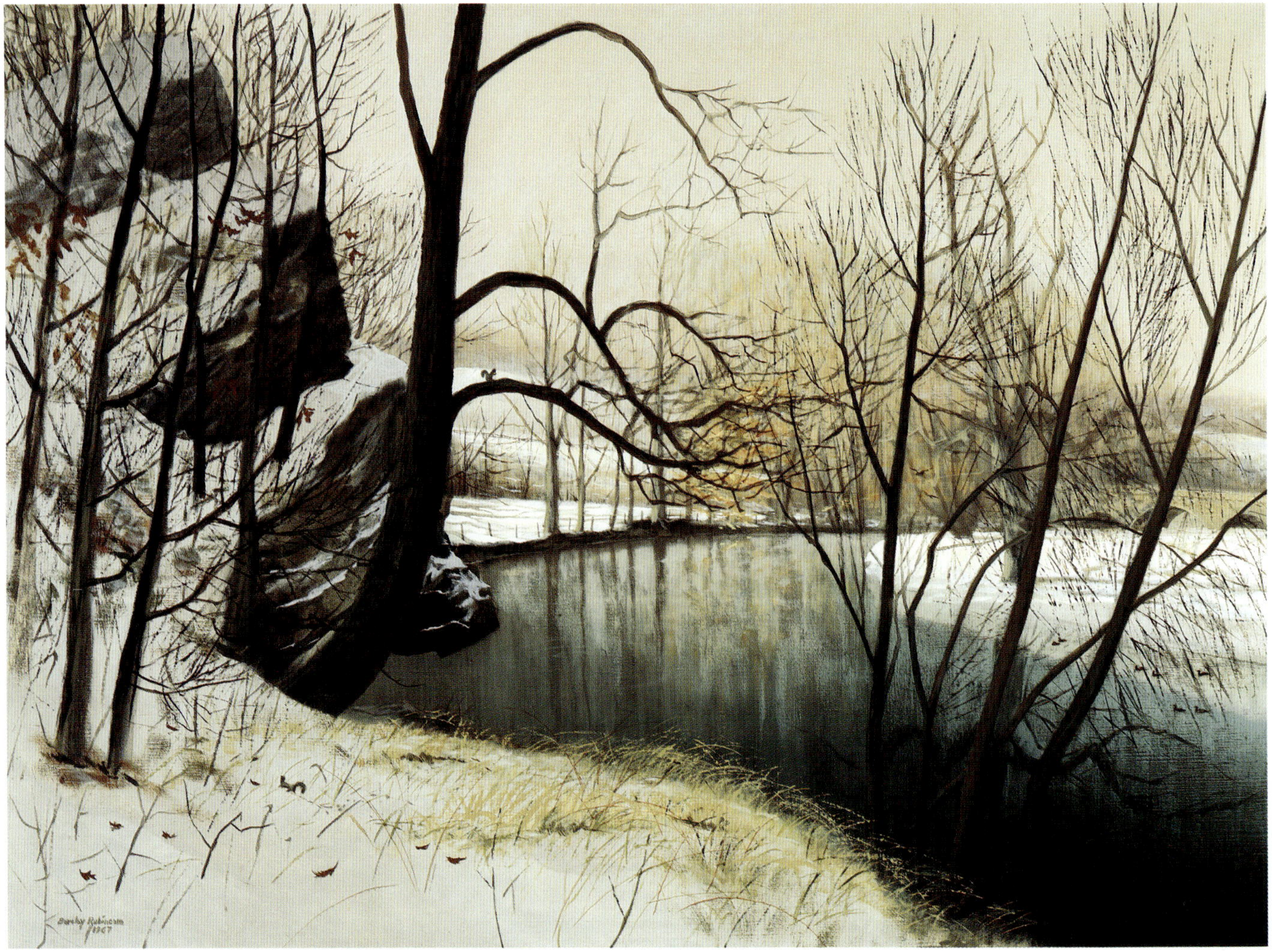

37. Deborah's Rock

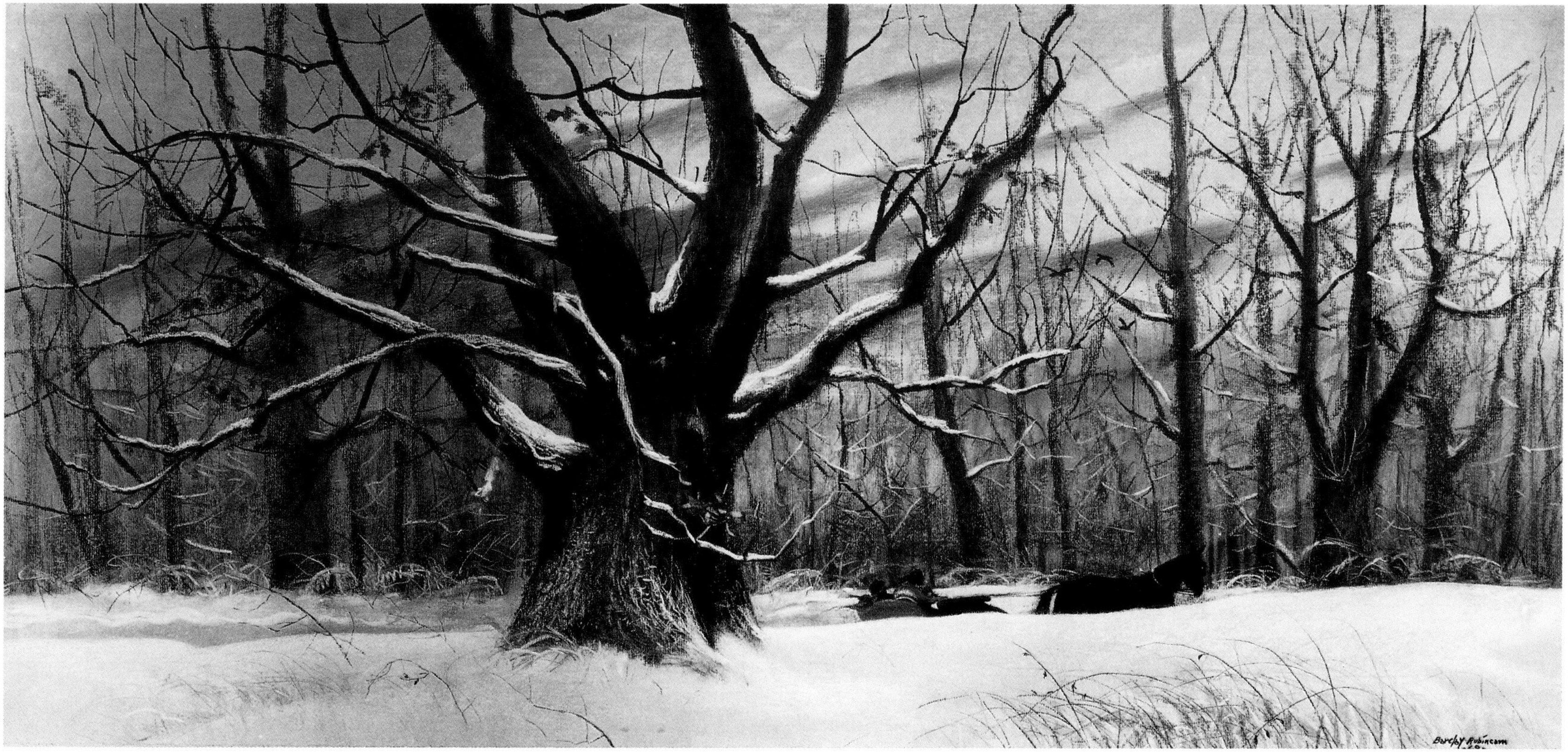

38. Sleigh Ride

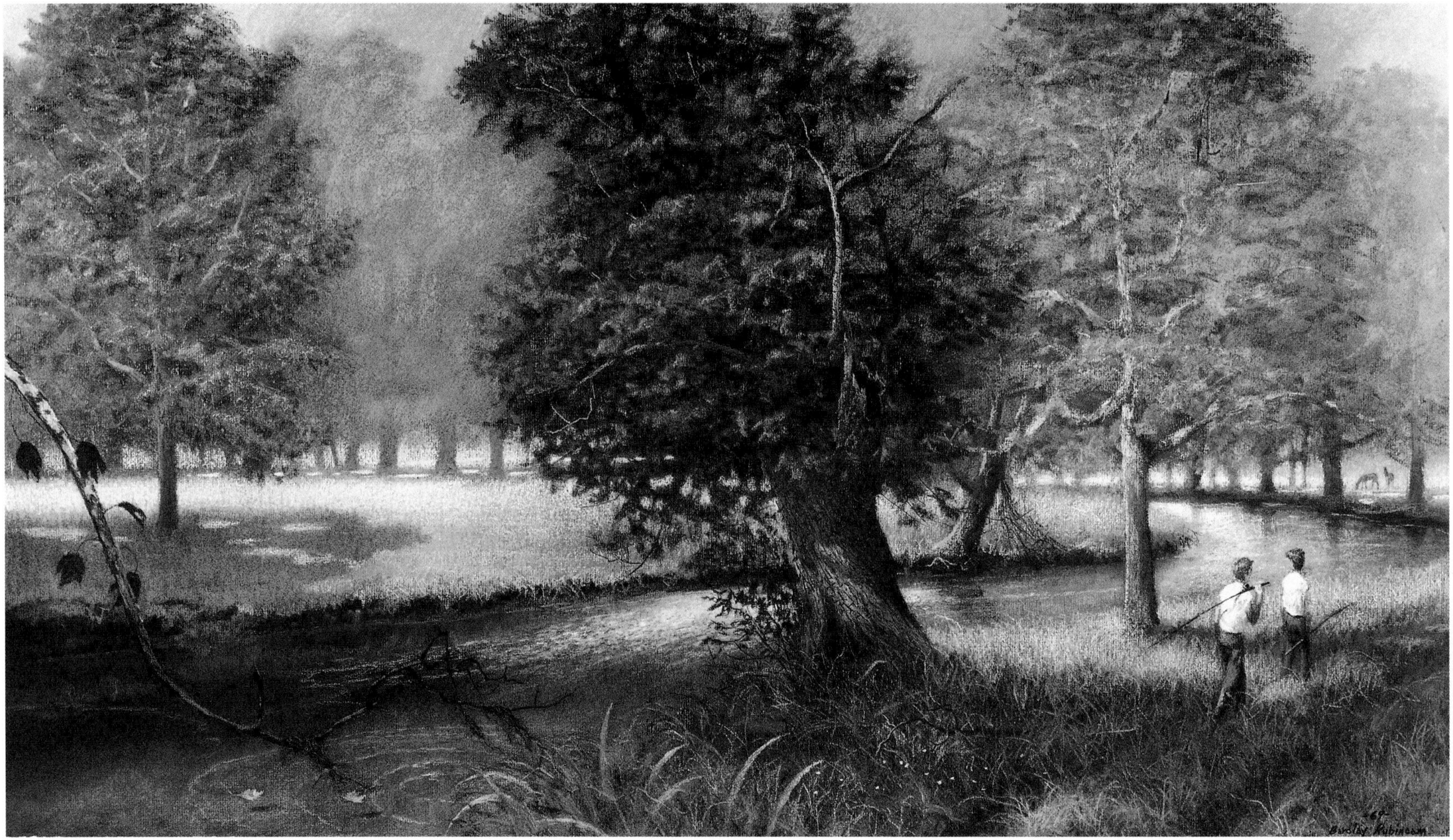

39. Boys Along the Brandywine

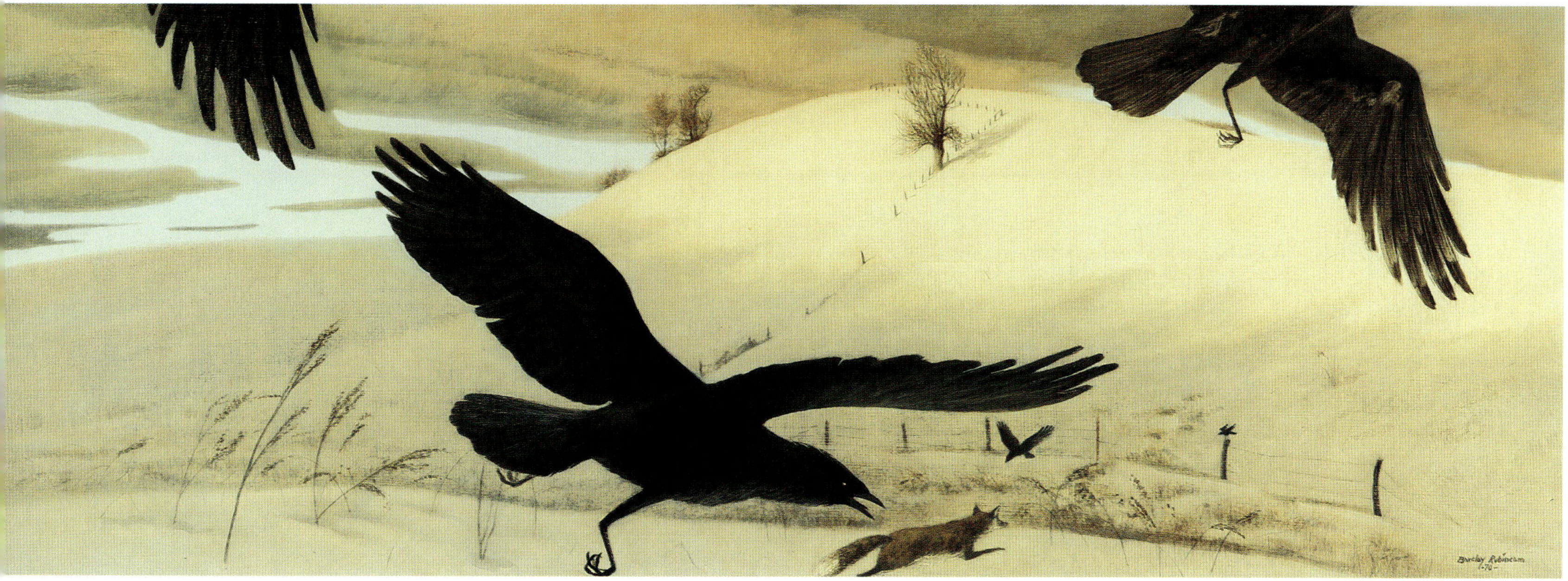

40. Early Morning in January

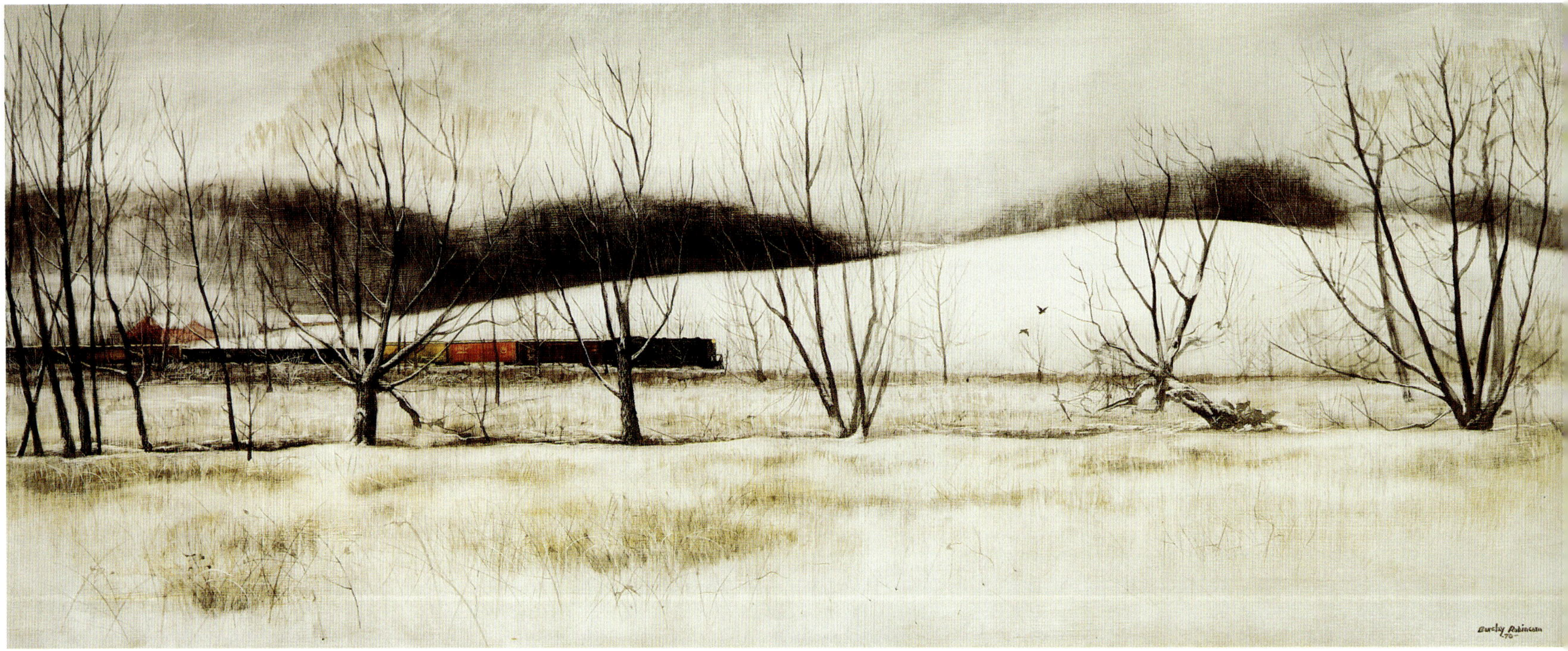

41. Freight Up from Wawaset

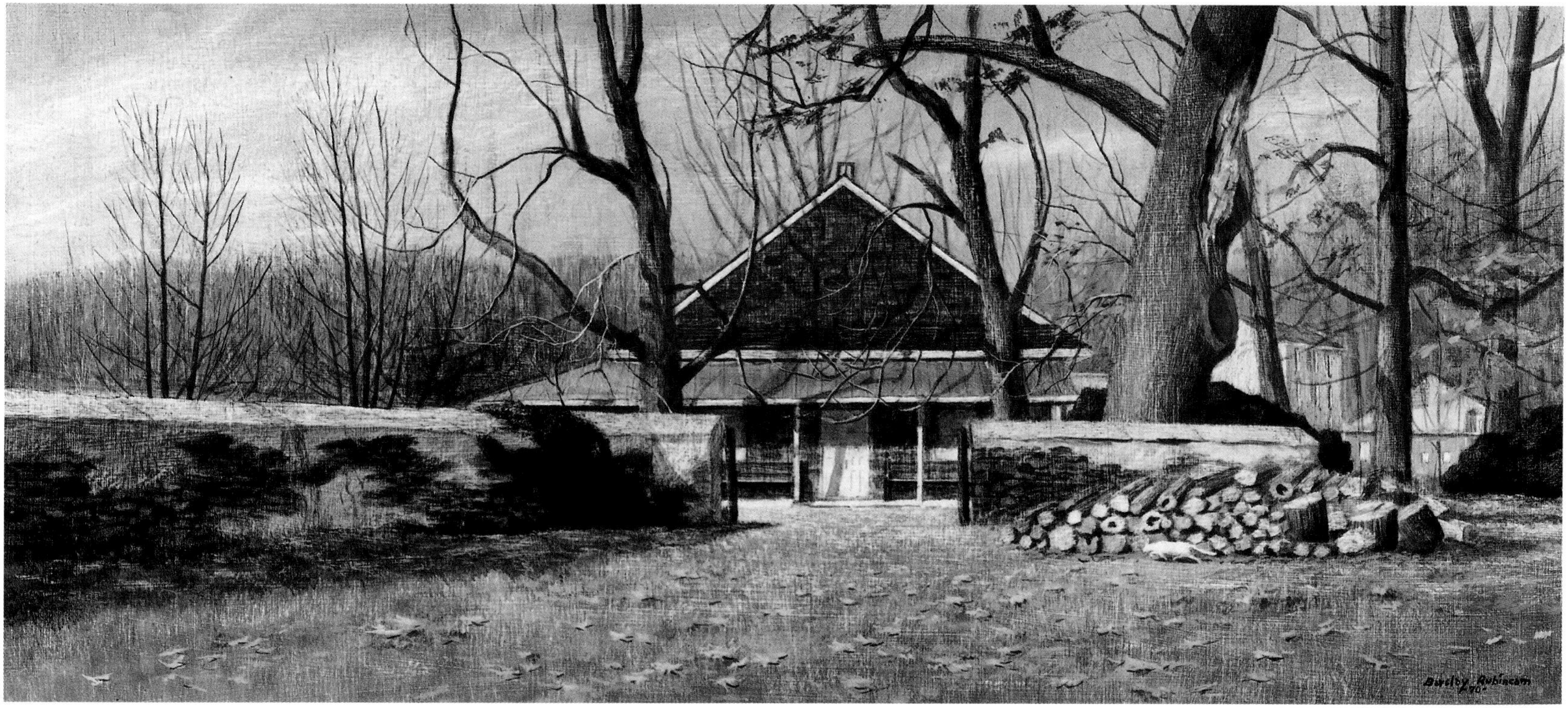

42. Bradford Friends Meeting

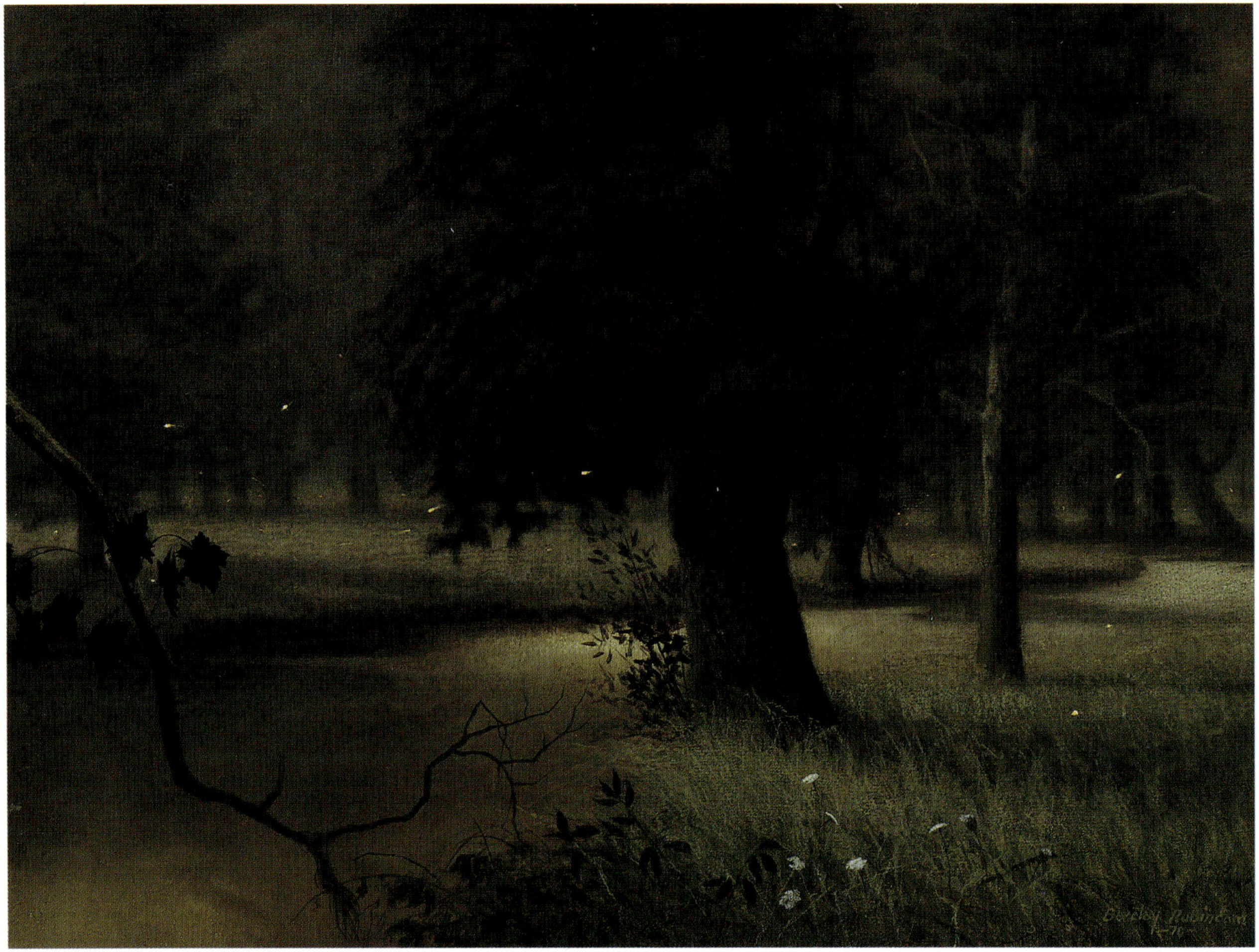

43. Moonlight on the Brandywine

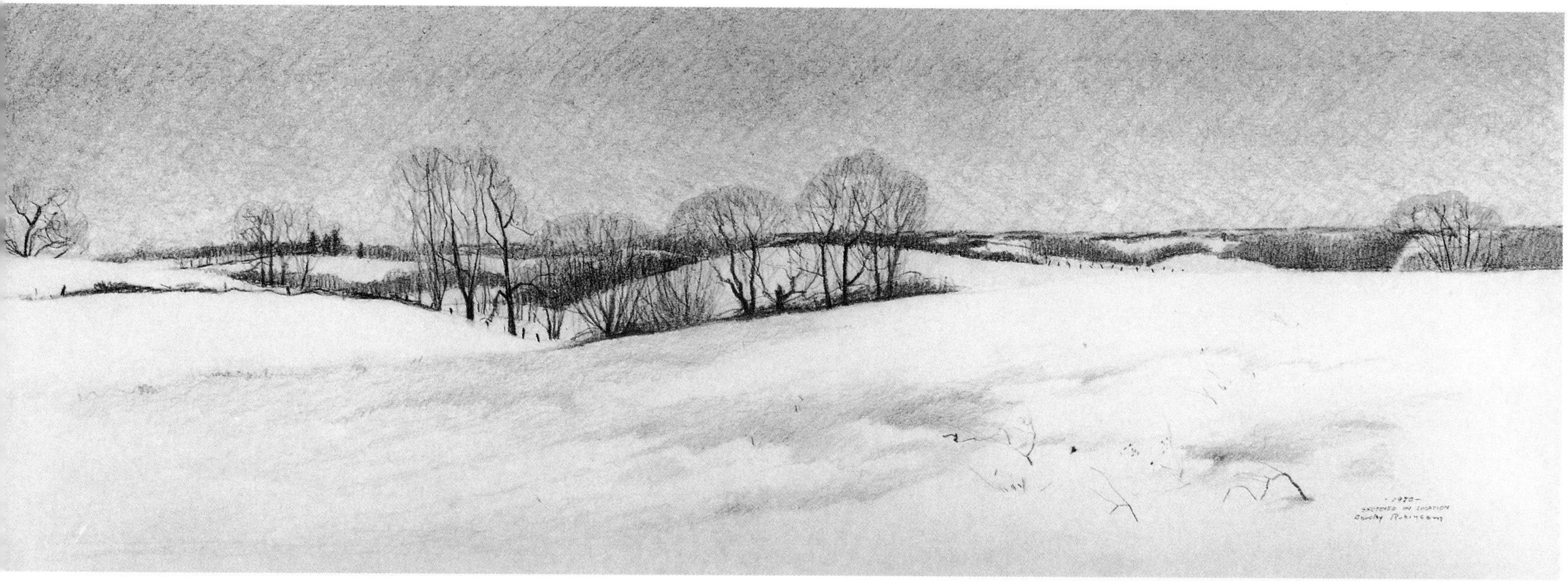

44. Landscape Sketch

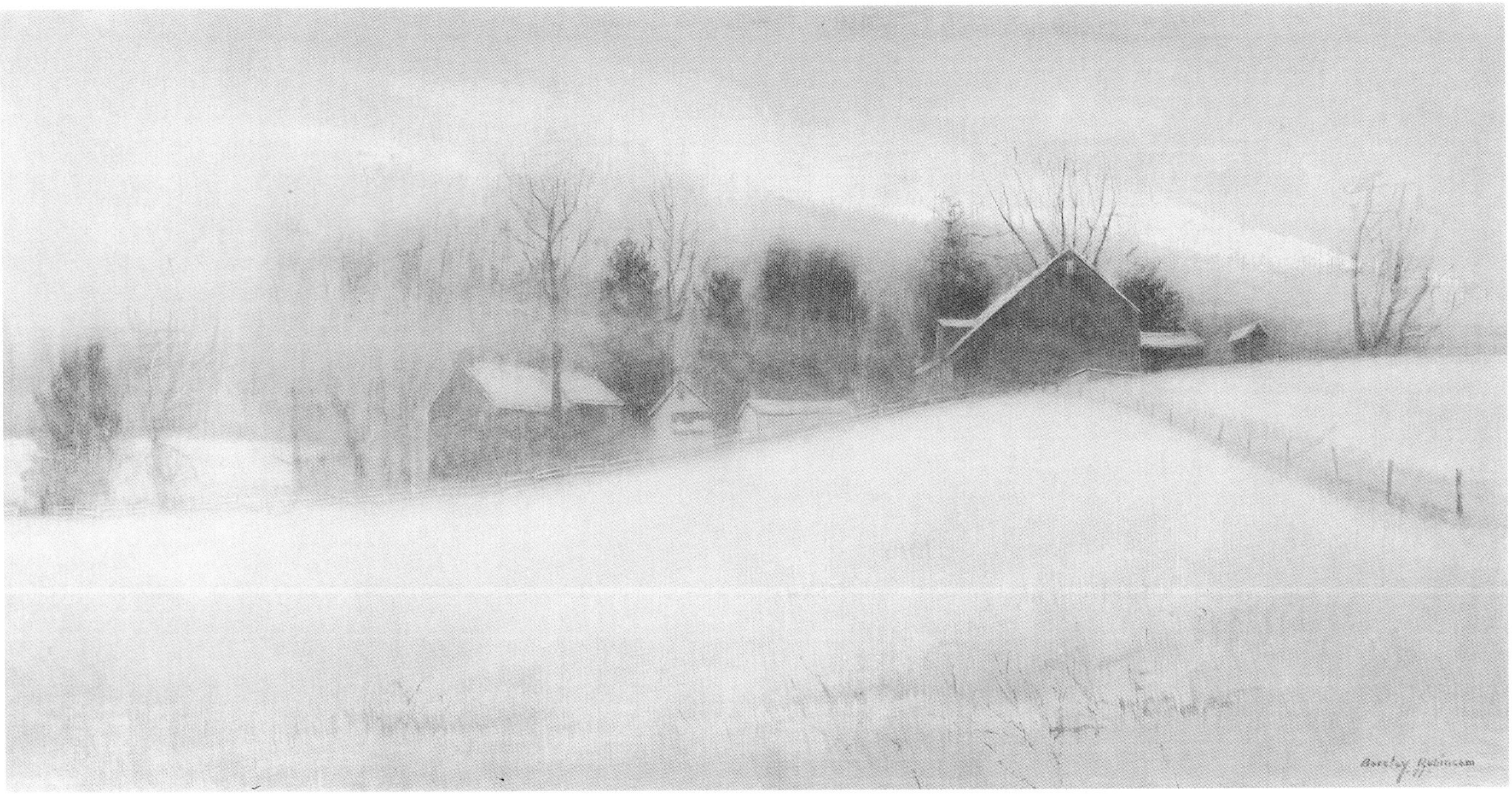

45. Homestead Near
Birmingham

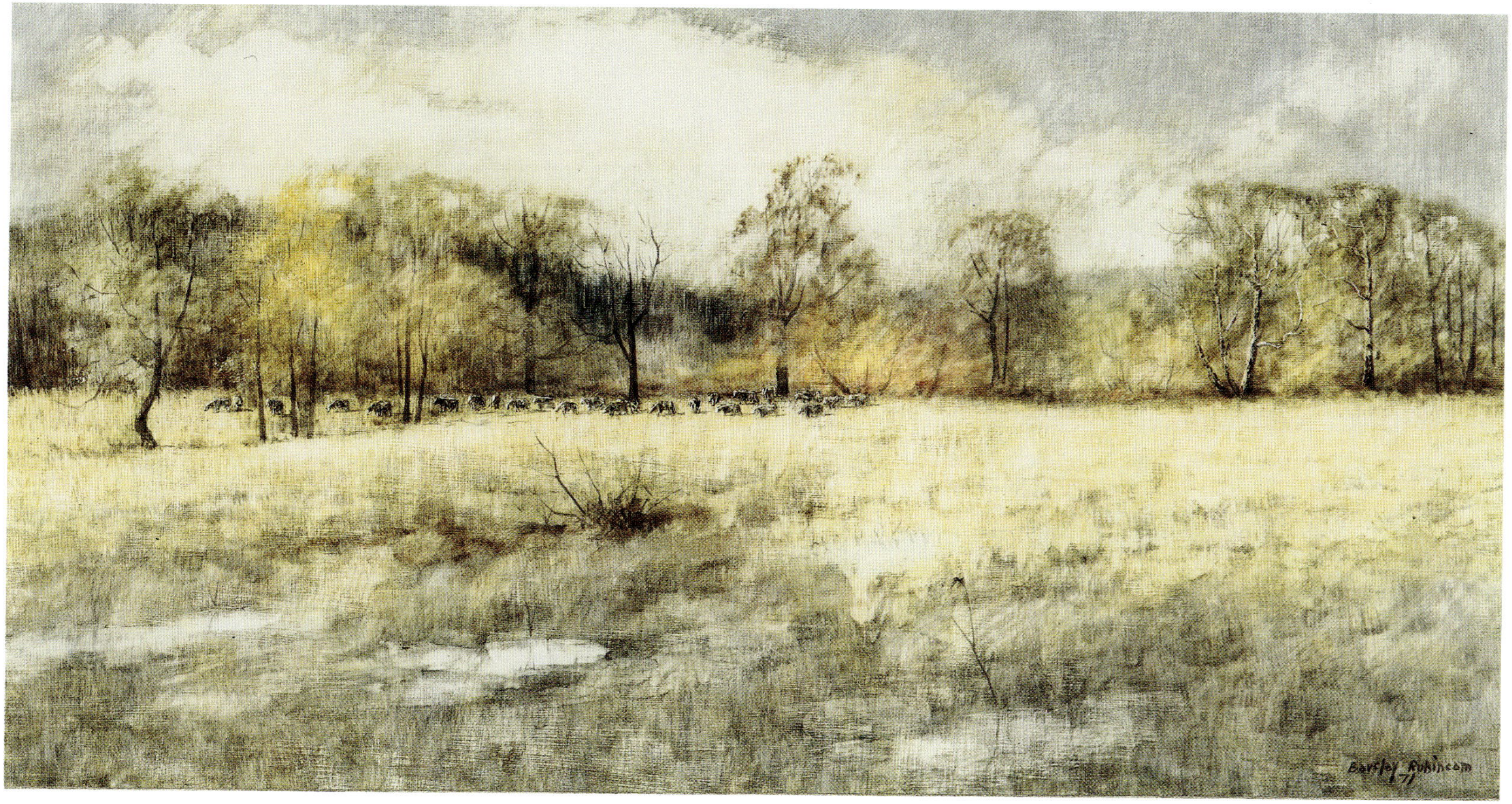

46. Sunrise on the
Brandywine Meadow

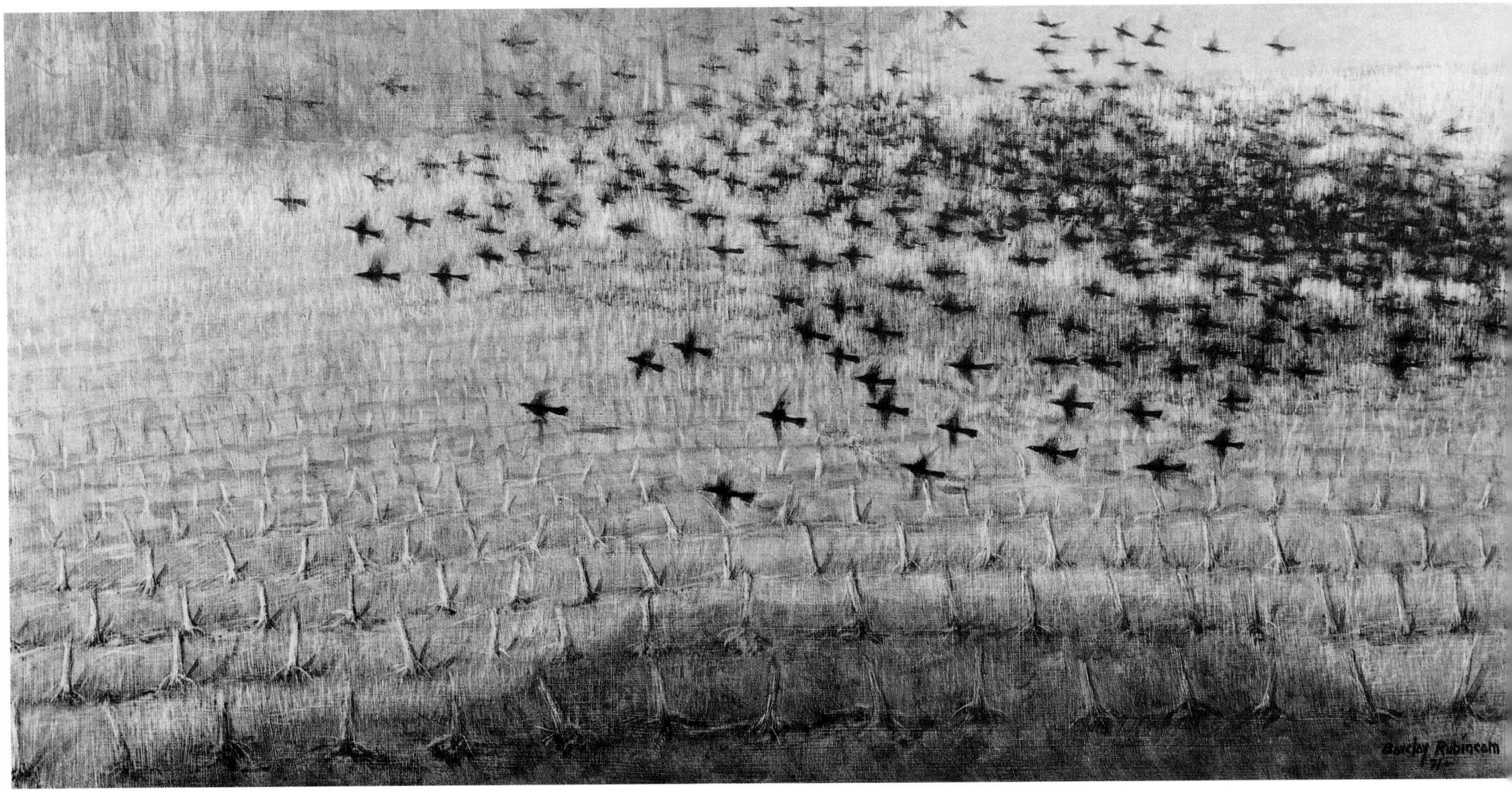

47. From the Car Window

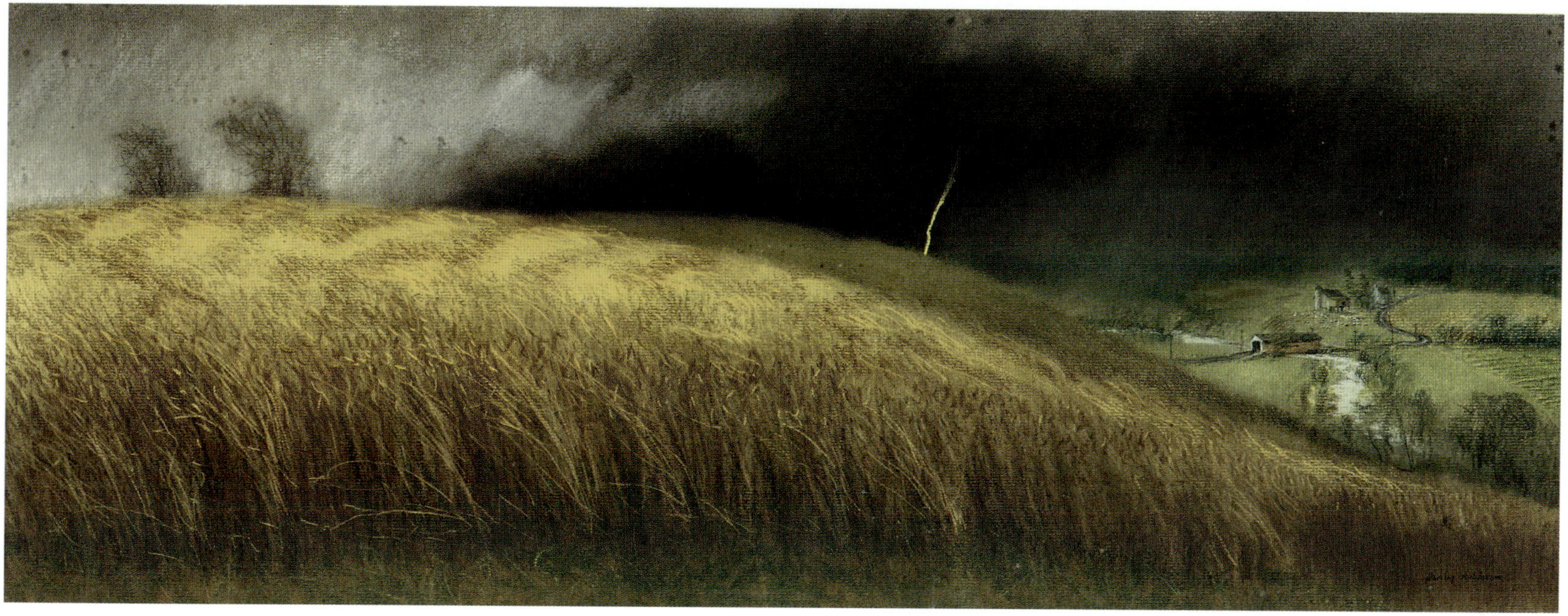

48. July Storm

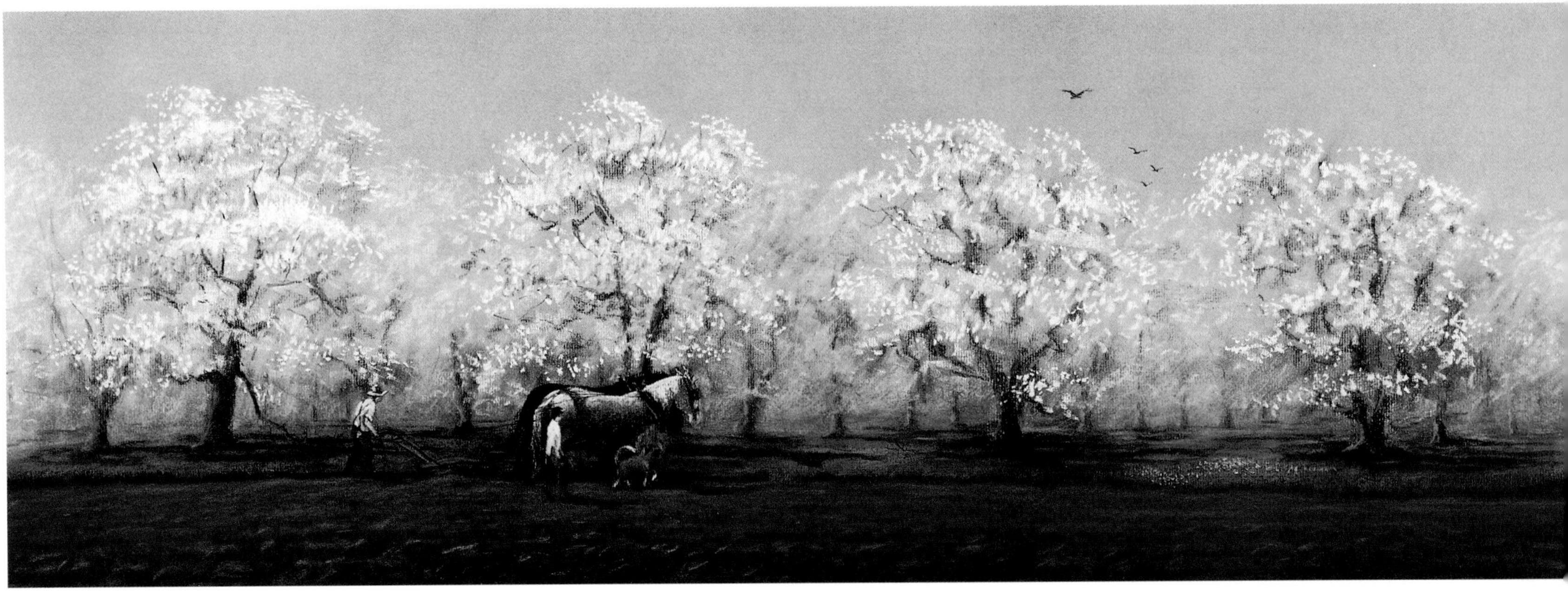

49. Plowing Time

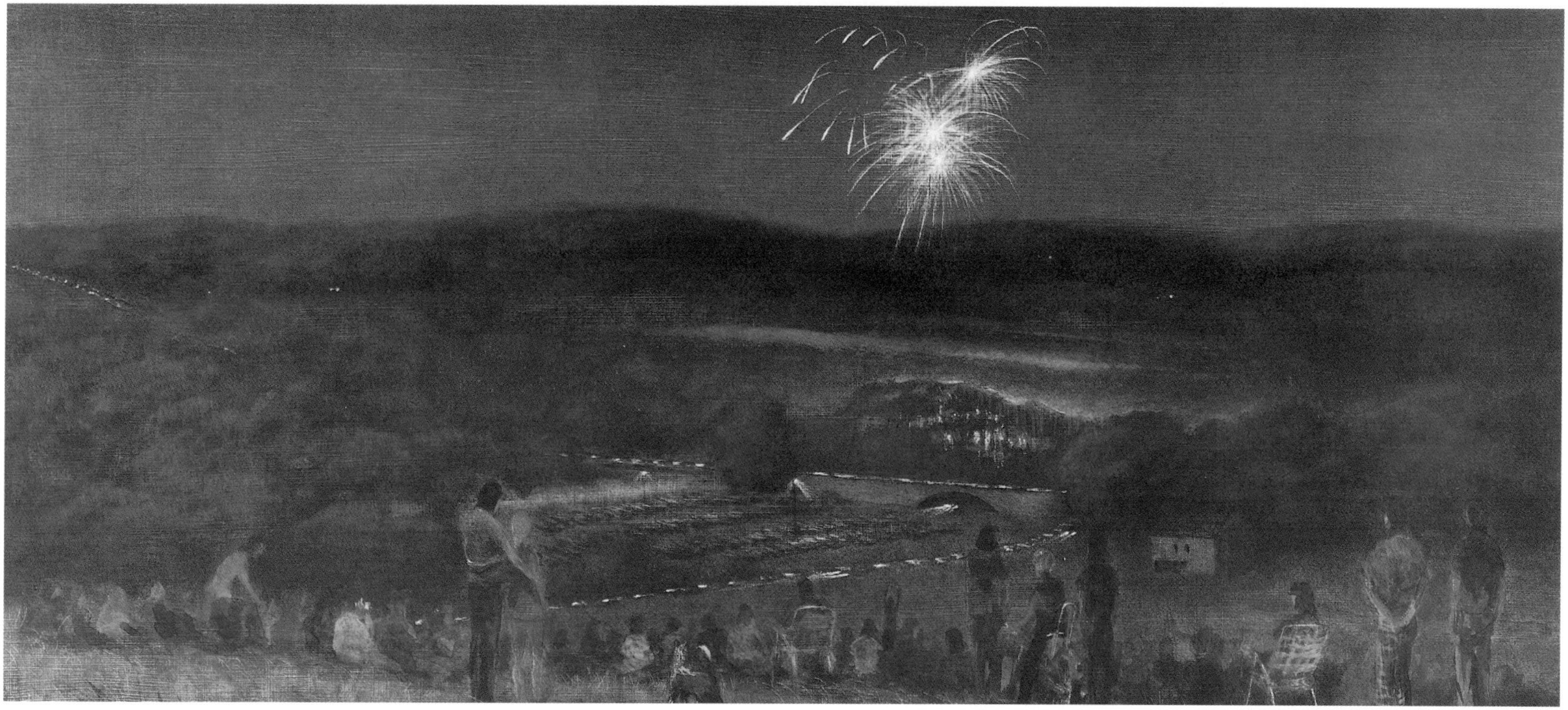

50. Fireworks – Fourth of July, Looking Out Over Lenape

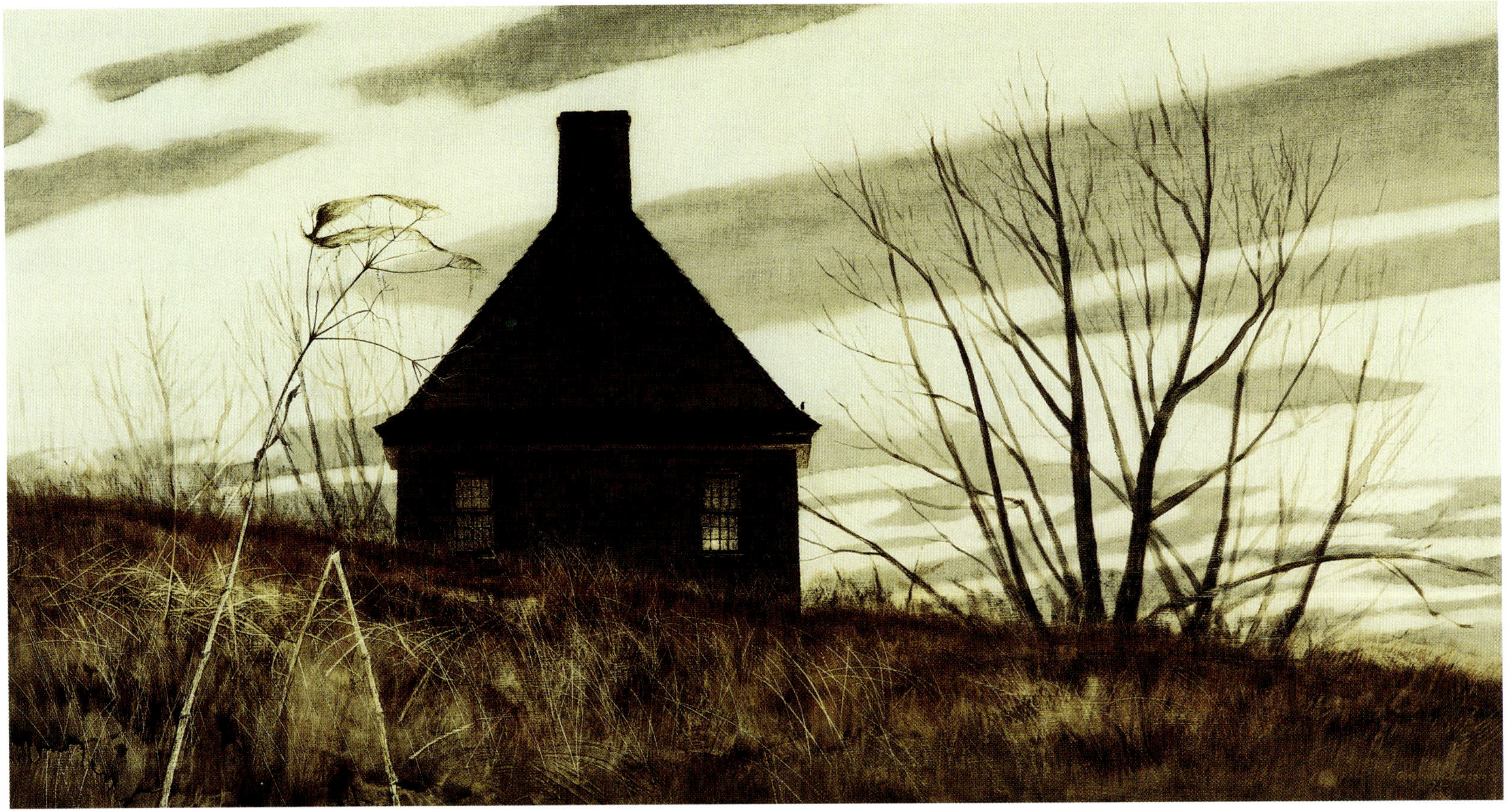

51. Pewter Country

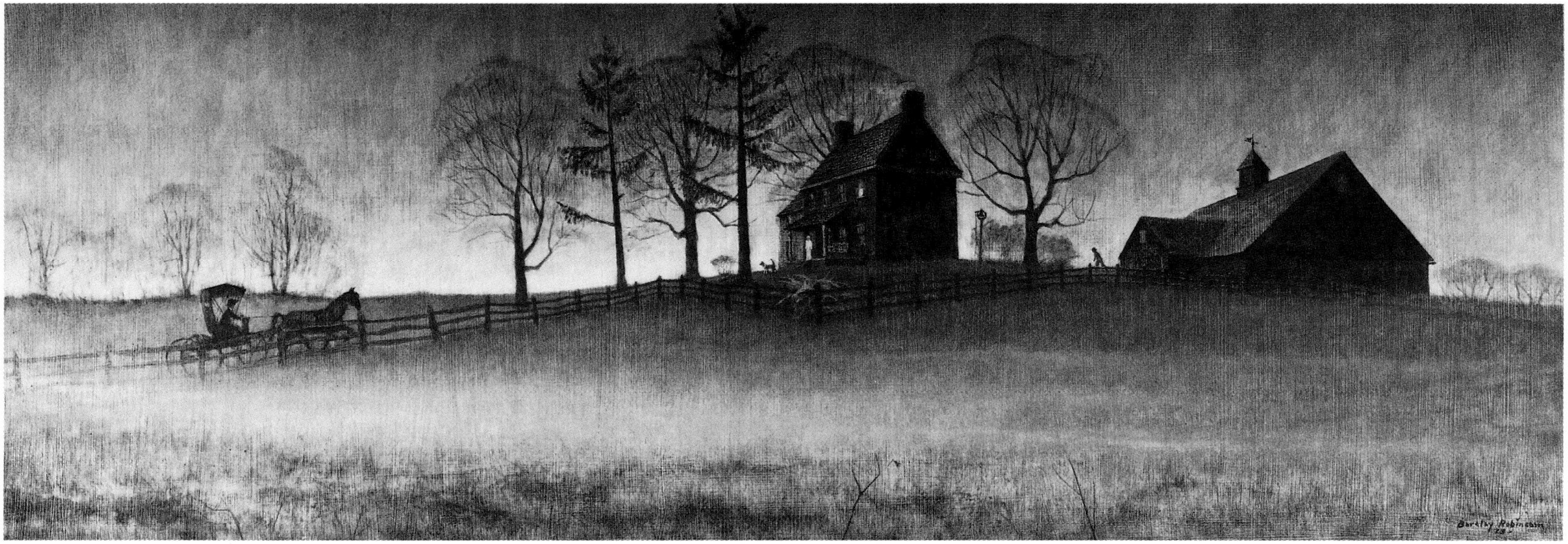

52. The Country Doctor's Visit

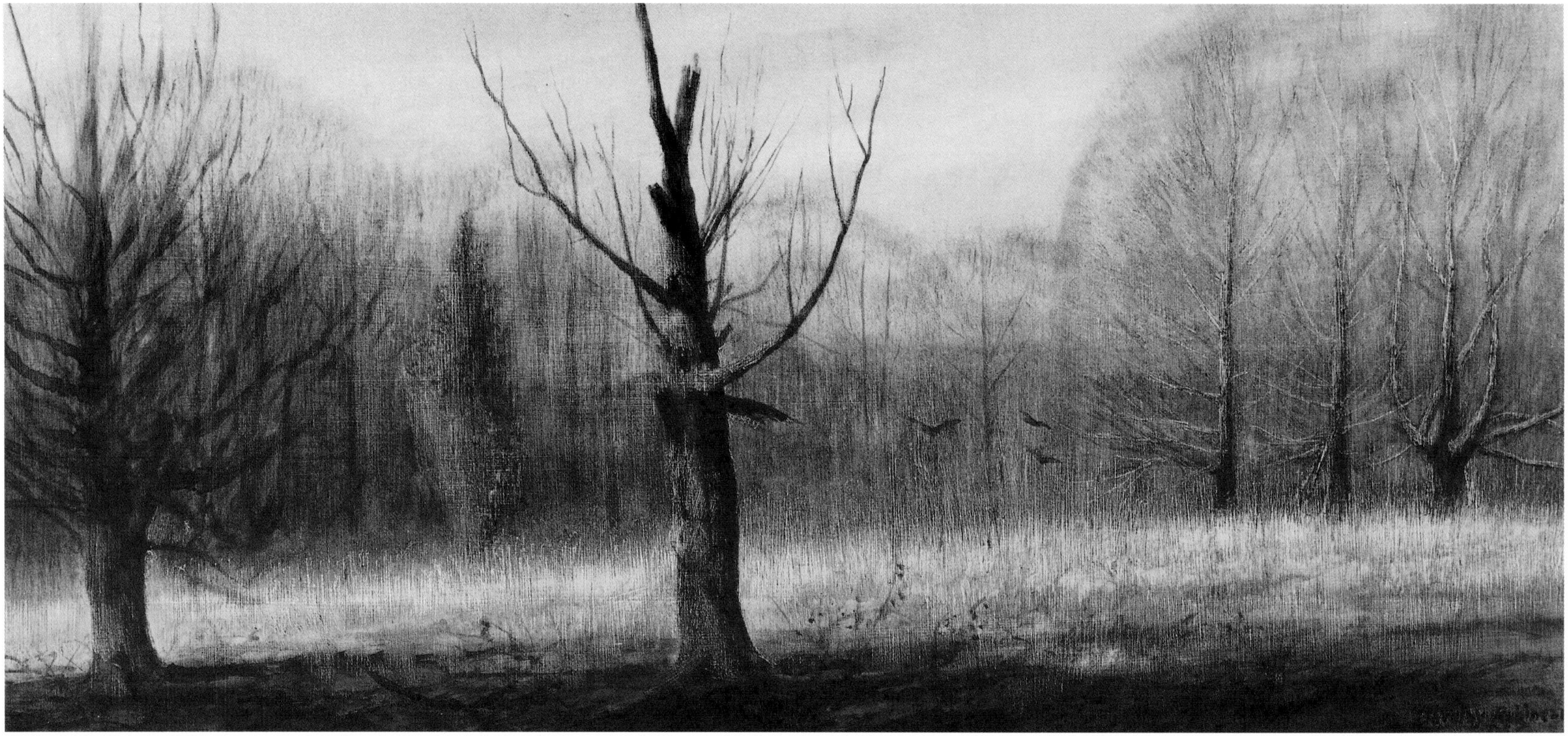

53. Late Afternoon on
Brandywine Battlefield

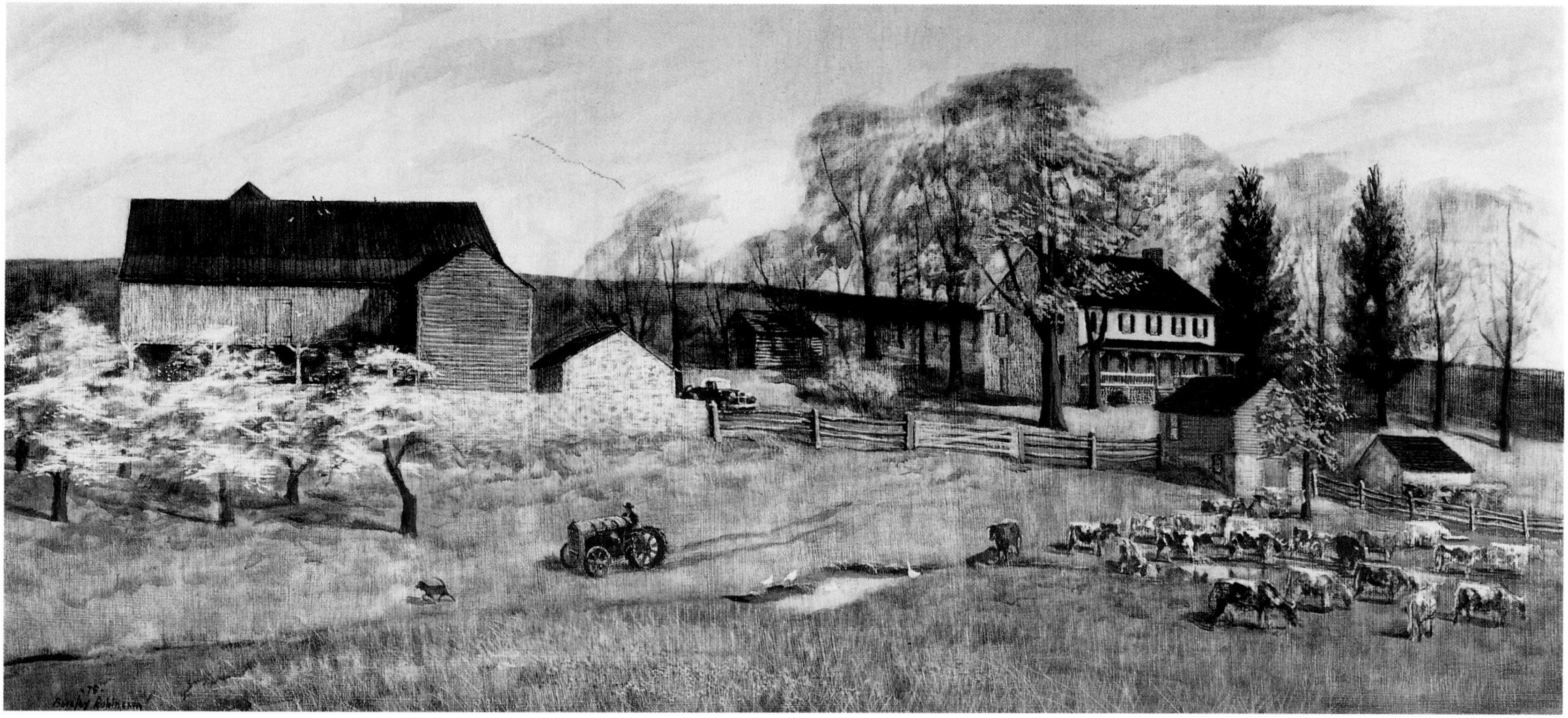

54. Memories of Our Farm

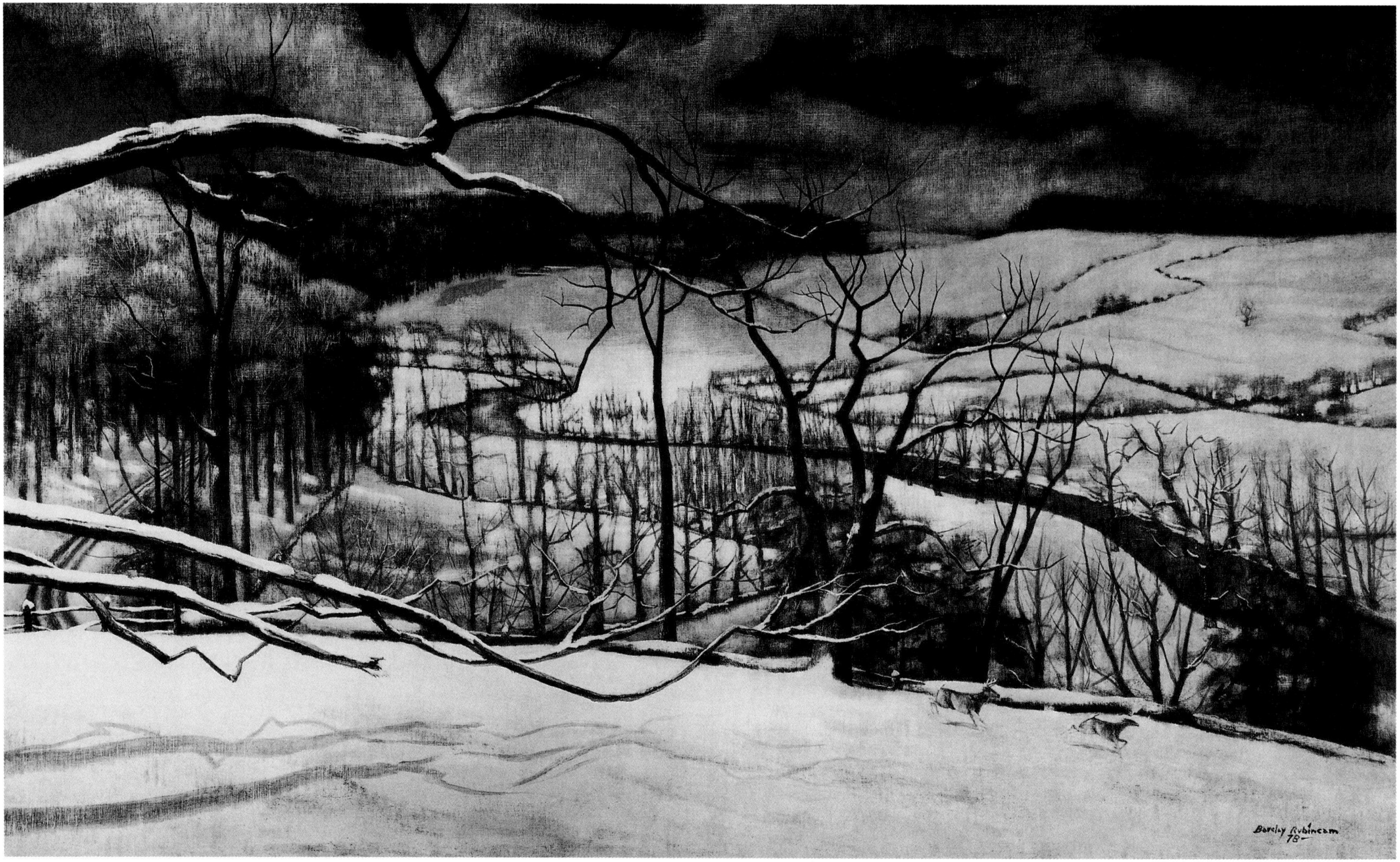

55. Sconnelltown Hill

Still Life Paintings

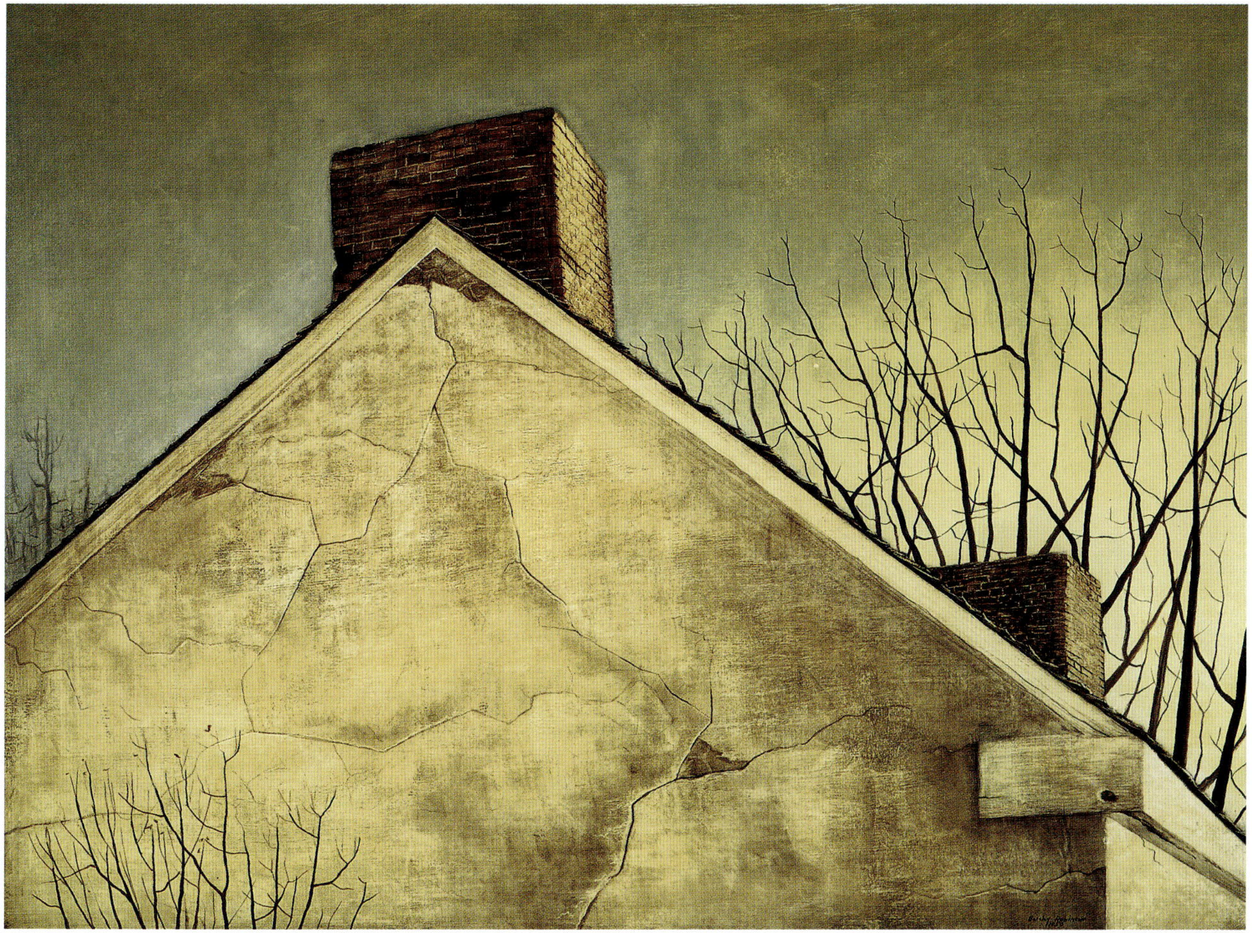

56. Generations

Rubincam's still life paintings are among his finest works. They demonstrate a strong sense of design, often illustrating a mastery of geometric composition. Each painting presents a close-up view of a familiar object – a family rocking chair, an antique chest, a child's toy – which is transformed by its setting. The isolated object takes on a kind of heightened reality, suggesting meaning and significance that far exceeds its physical appearance.

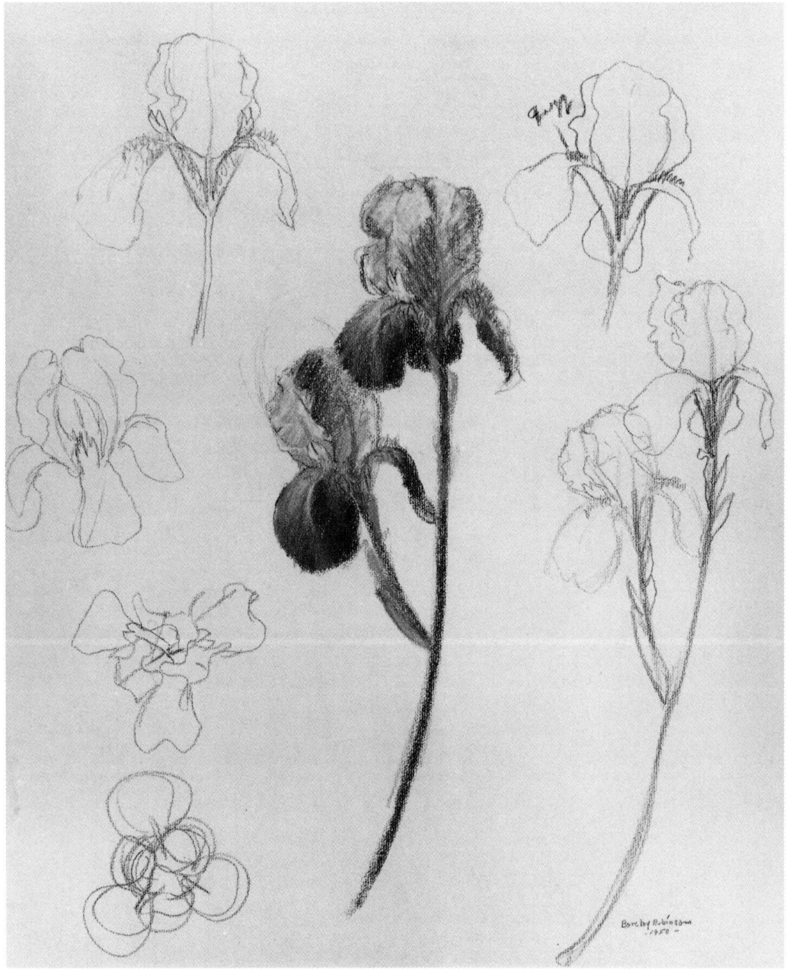

57. Iris

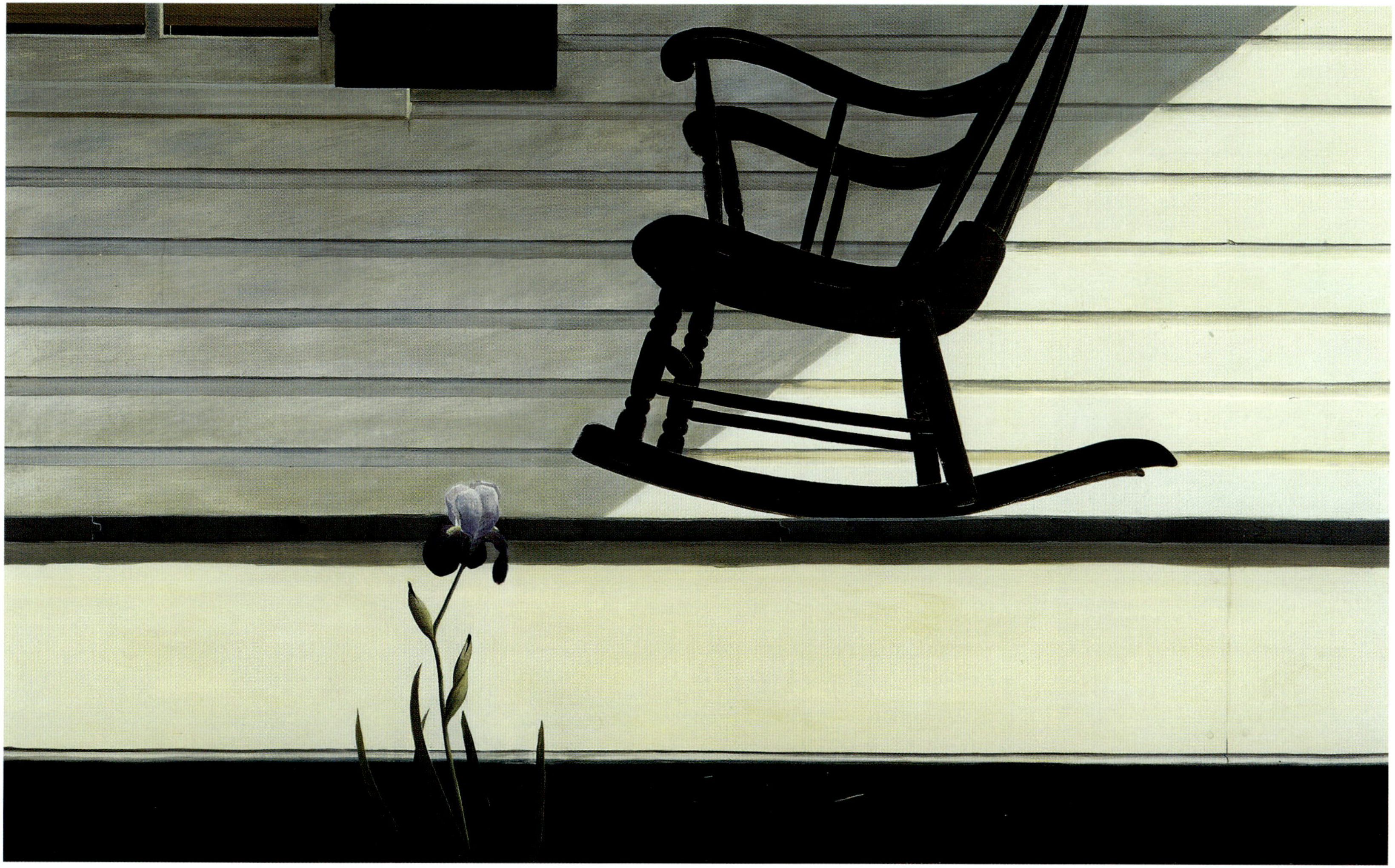

58. Memorial Day

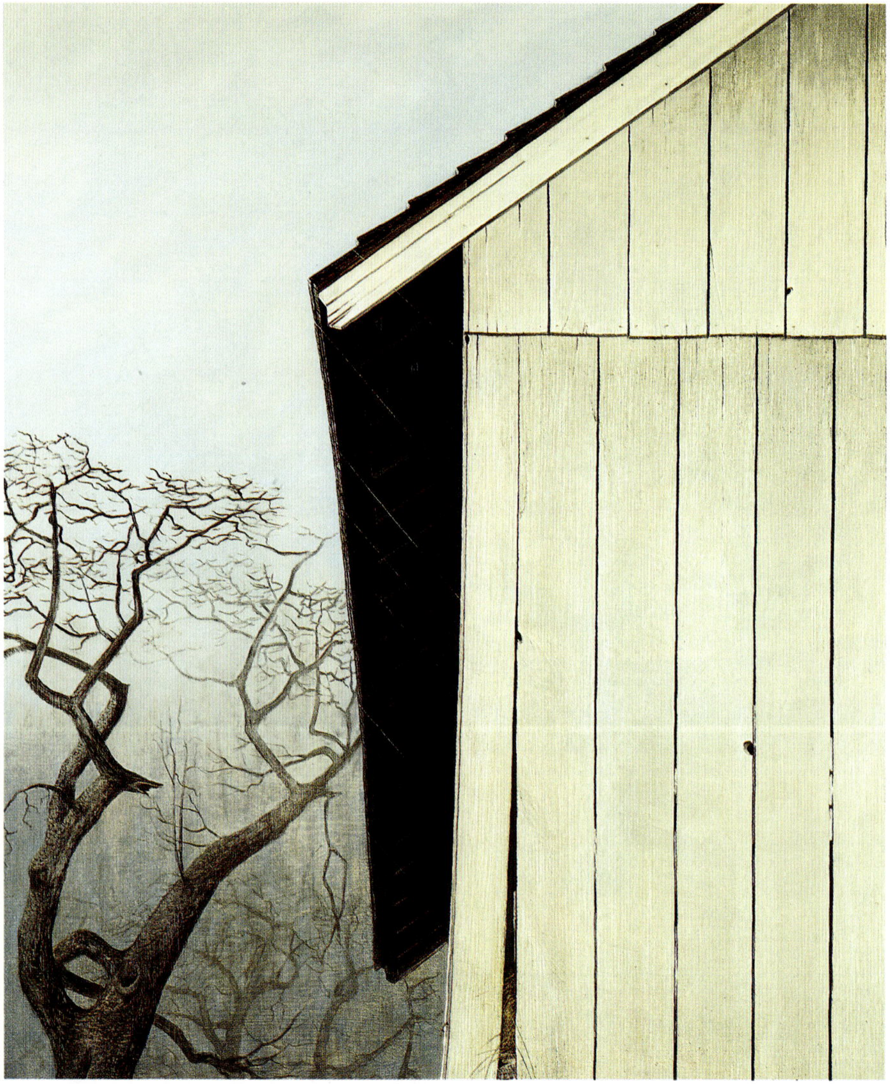

59. It's Raining

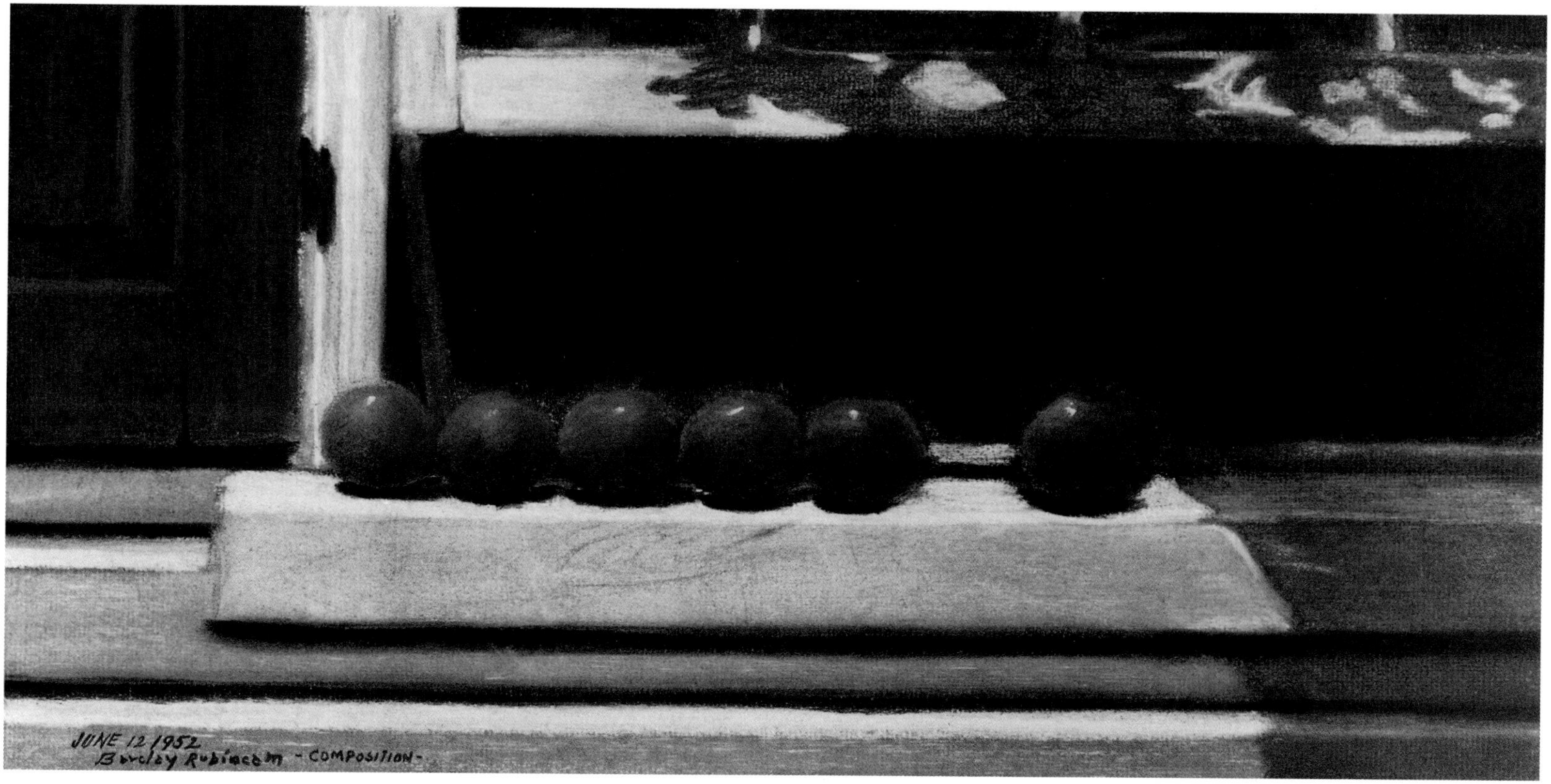

60. Ripe Tomatoes

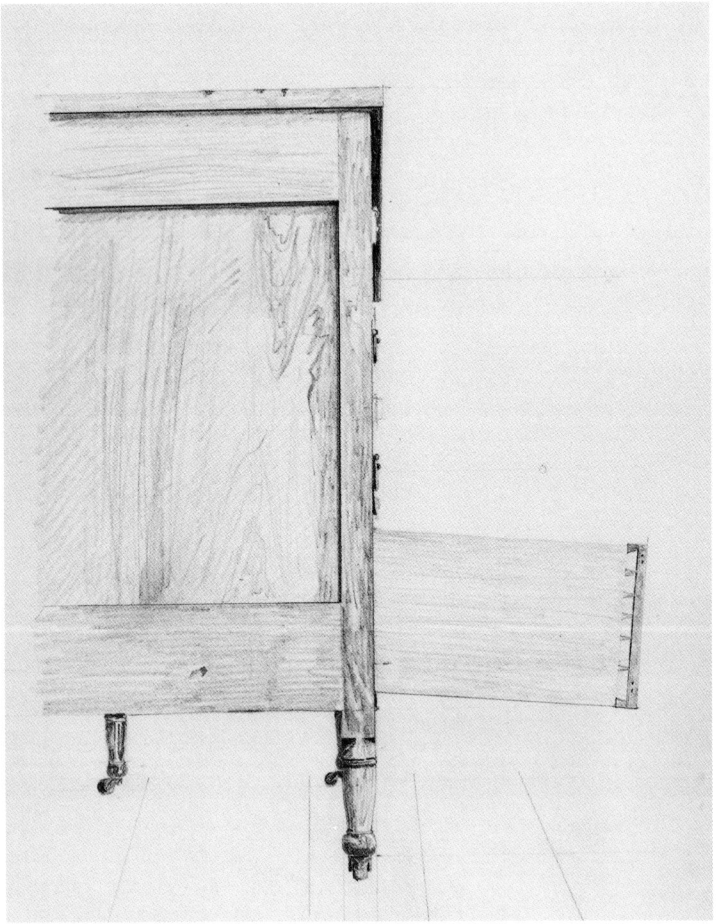

61. Sketch for The Open
Drawer

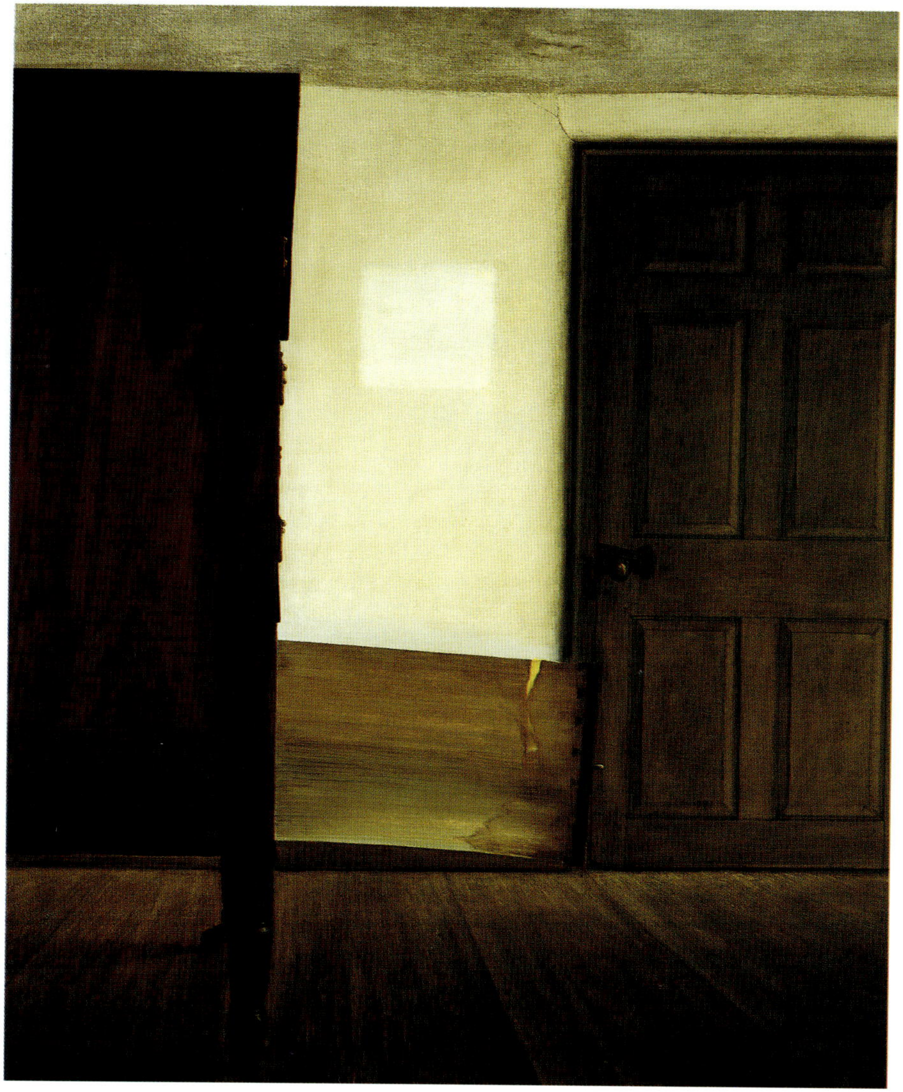

62. The Open Drawer

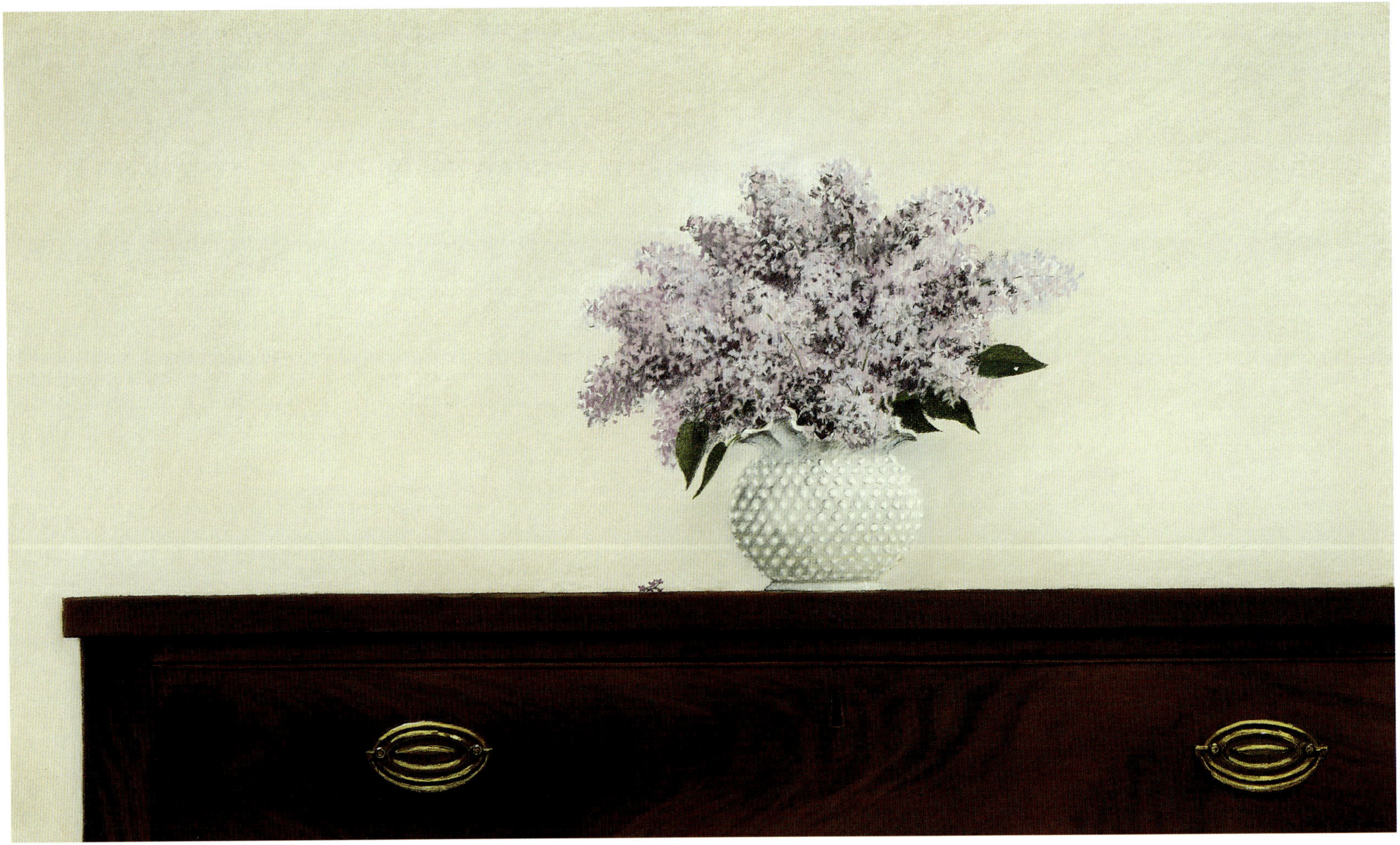

63. Lilacs on a Chest

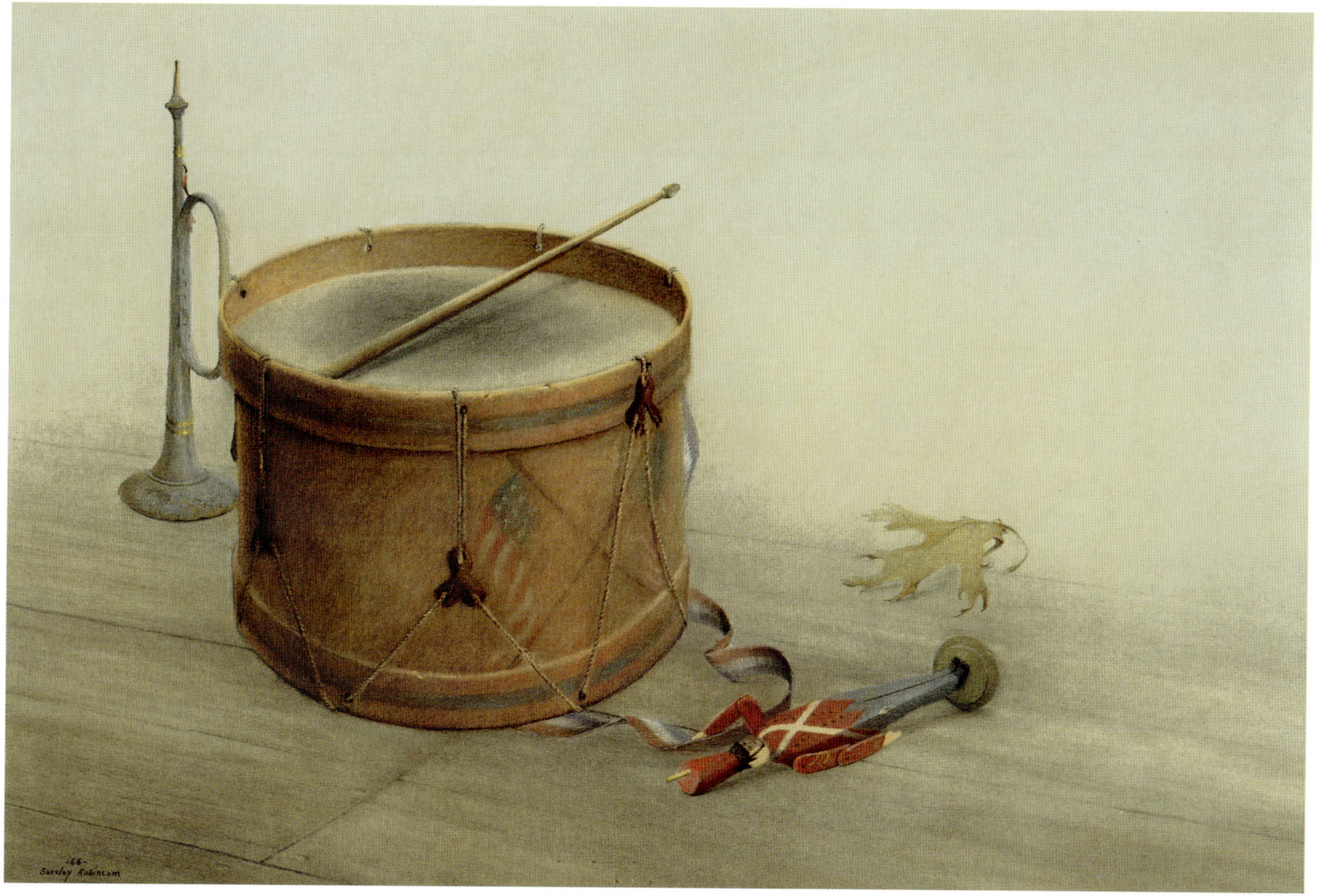

64. "The Fallen Soldier"

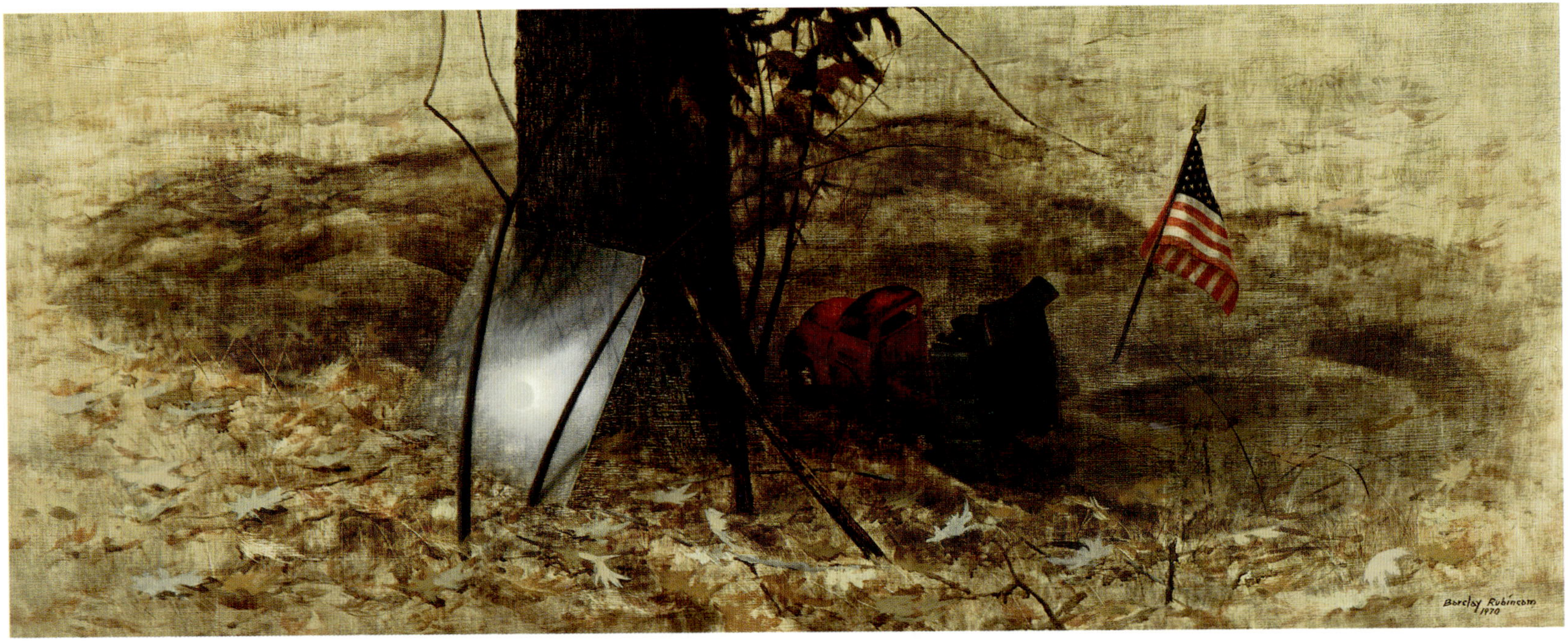

65. The Day of the Eclipse

Portraits

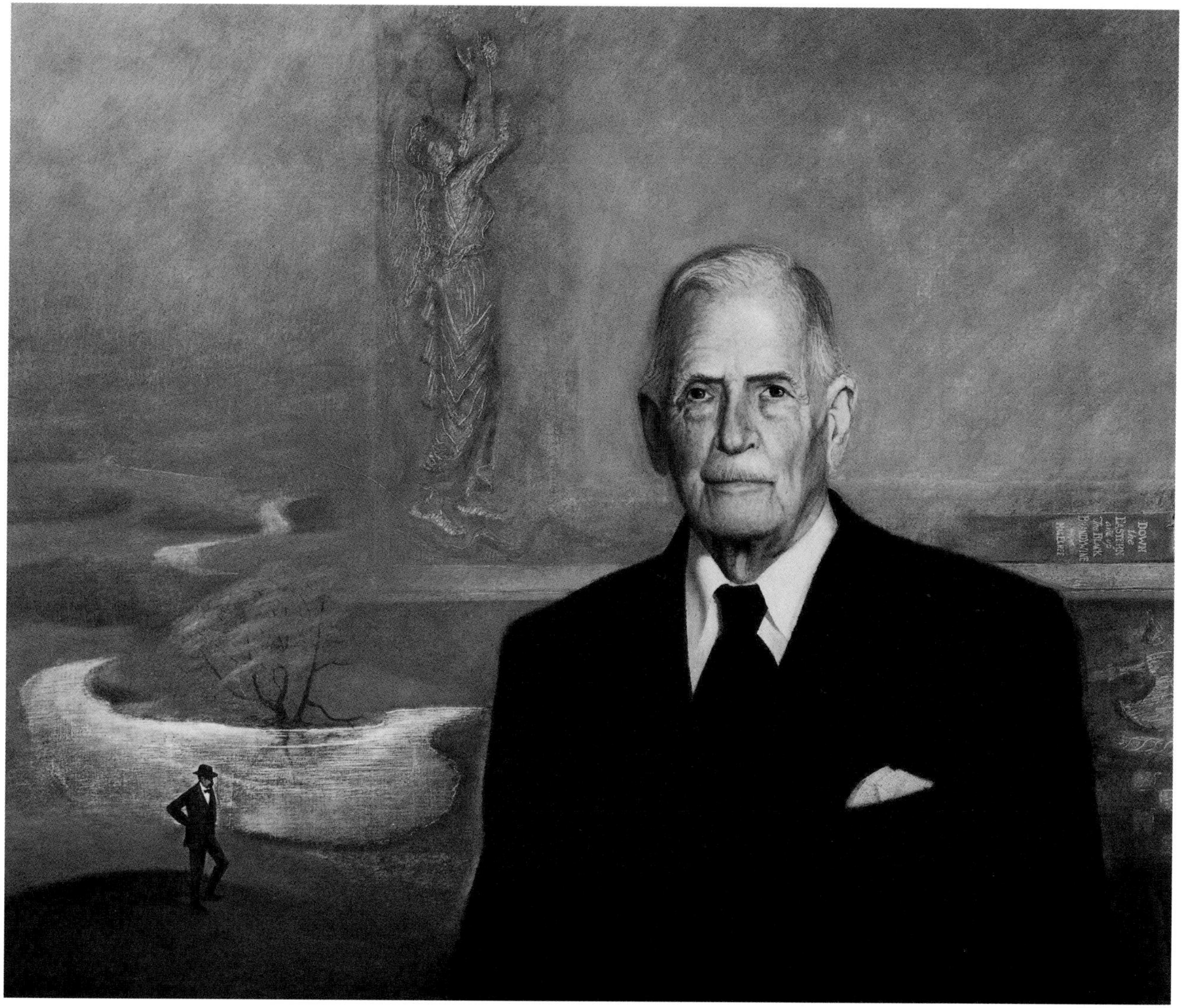

Barclay Rubincam's portraits are candid and direct. Each subject gazes at the viewer with the ease and familiarity of a friend. Many portraits also extend Rubincam's interest in combining past and present. The sitter may be seen in a contemporary moment but is often surrounded by symbols drawn from his or her personal history. Such portraits are at once both physical appearance and record of an accomplished life.

66. Portrait of Wilmer W. MacElree

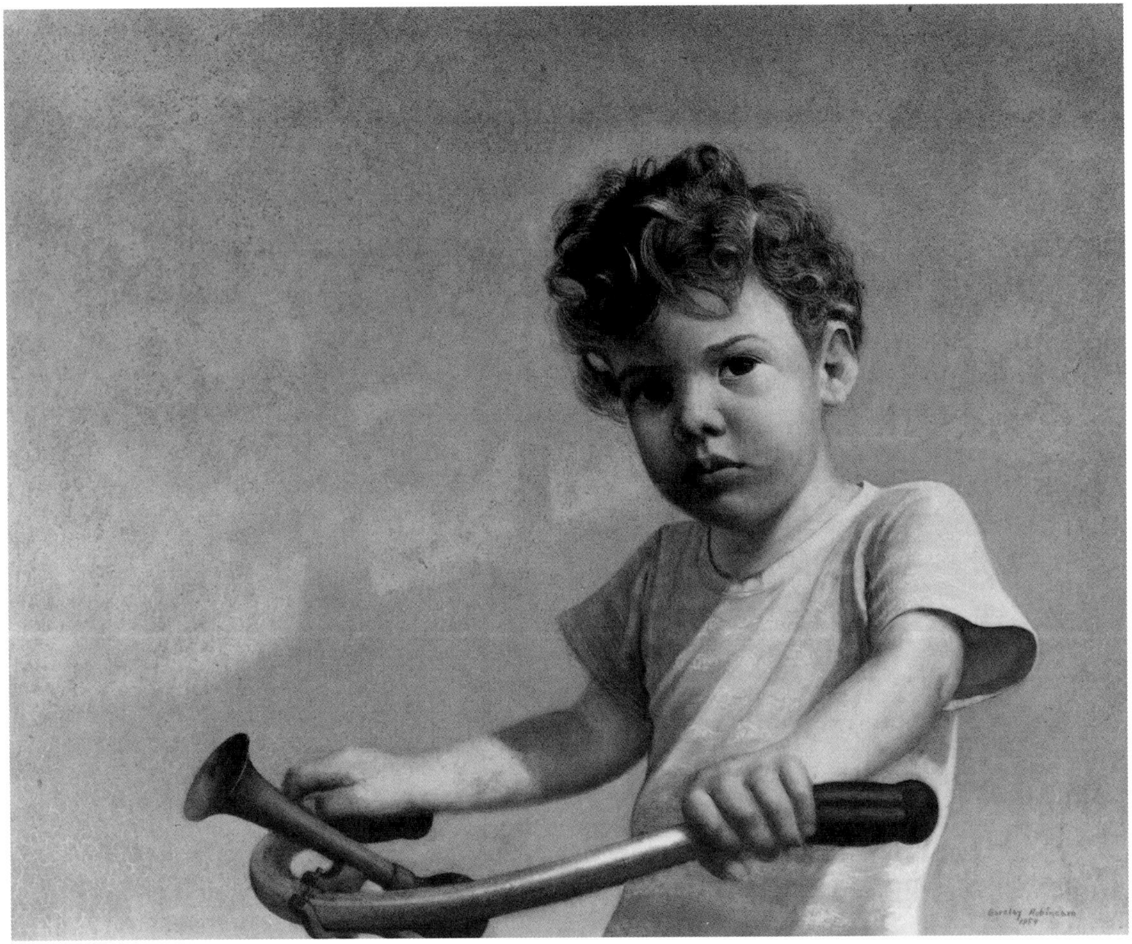

67. Portrait of André
(Age 2 1/2)

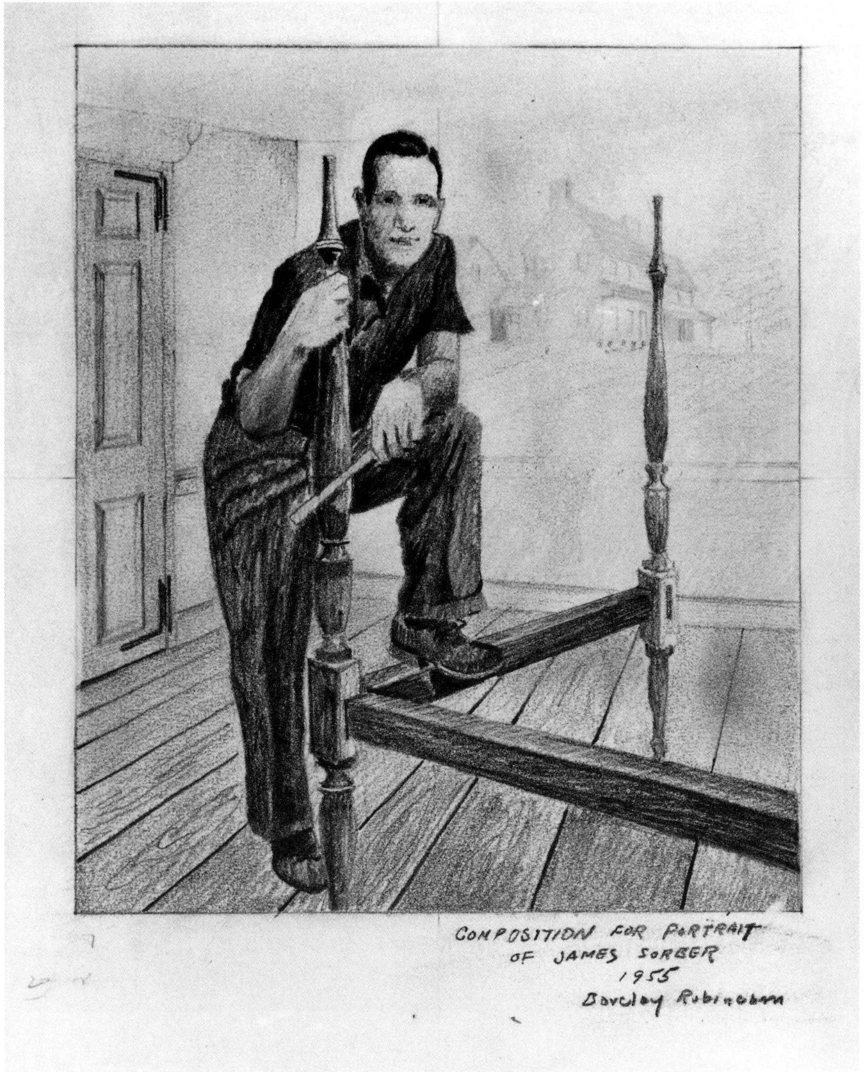

68. Study for The Collector

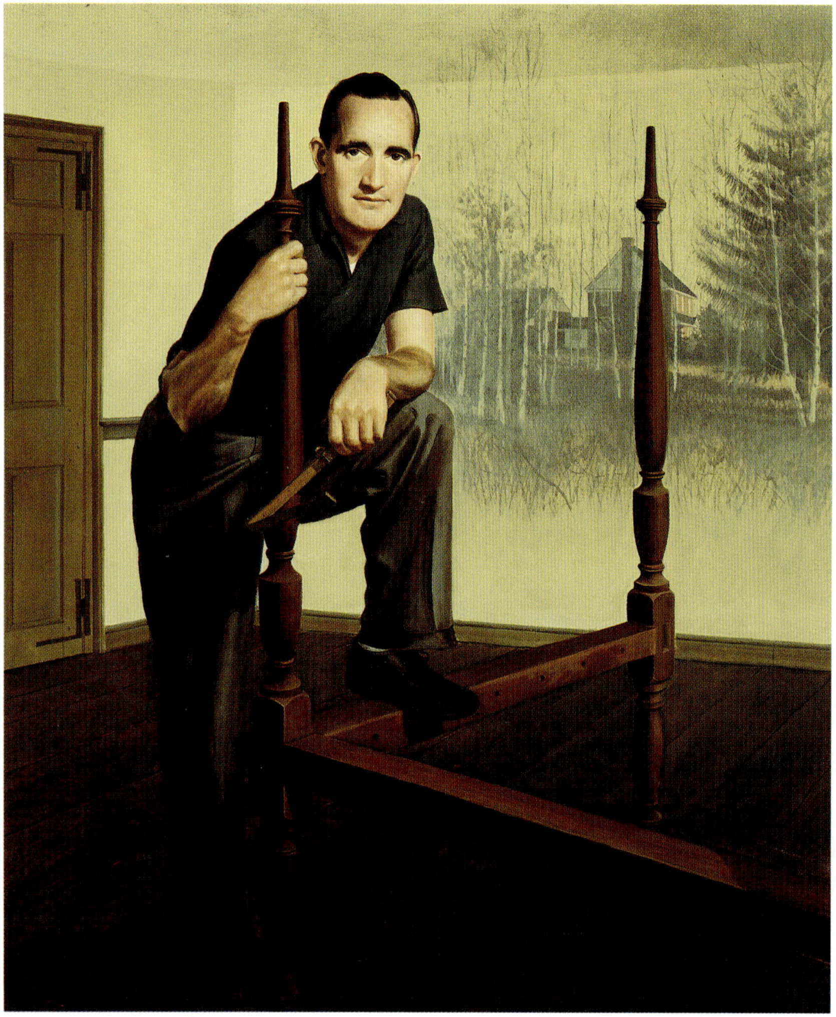

69. The Collector (Portrait of James C. Sorber)

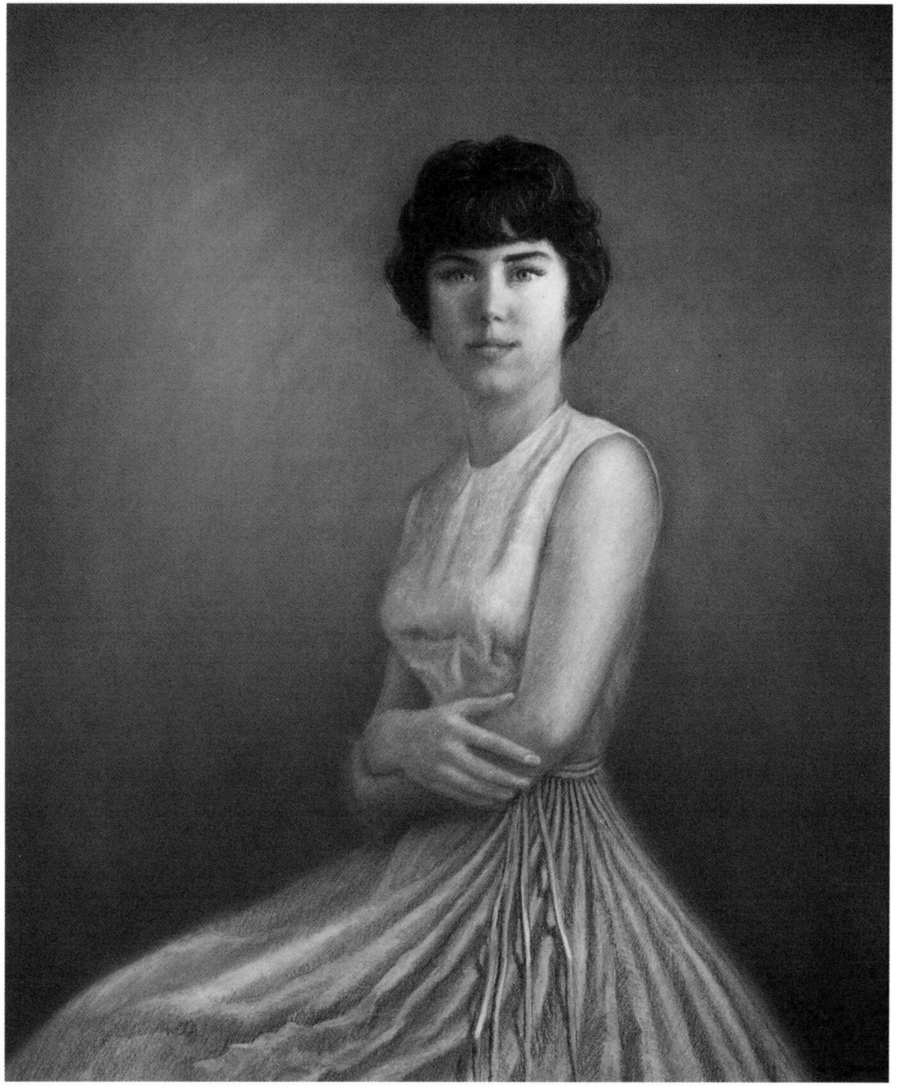

70. Portrait of Nelda Jane Davis

Catalogue of the Exhibition

Catalogue entries are arranged under topical headings. The artist's title for a work appears in bold. Alternate titles (some used by the artist, some given by owners) and explanatory notes appear in brackets. Within a topical heading, works are arranged in chronological order according to the artist's dates. Undated works are so noted. Medium notations are based on the artist's notes. Composition measurements are in inches, height preceding width. Lenders' names appear in italics.

Early Work

1. Spring Plowing 1940
1940
Oil on canvas
35 1/2 x 39 1/2
Mrs. Barclay Rubincam

2. Yank Correspondent
1944
Pastel
29 1/2 x 21 1/2
Mrs. Barclay Rubincam

3. Kanaka Mother in White Turban
Undated, circa 1943
Pastel
22 1/2 x 18
Mrs. Barclay Rubincam

4. Sketches from New Caledonia [collage]
Undated, circa 1943
Pencil
Mrs. Barclay Rubincam

5. Sketches for Battle Scene Murals for War Information Center [collage]
Undated, circa 1943
Watercolor
Mrs. Barclay Rubincam

6. Ring of Autumn
1947
Oil on canvas
28 1/2 x 41 1/4
Private Collection

West Chester History

7. Looking North on High Street
1963
Oil on panel
29 1/4 x 47 1/2
Commonwealth Bank

8. At the Turn of the Century
1965
Oil on canvas
29 5/8 x 47 1/2
John and Lisa Hall

9. Old Main
1968
Pastel
22 1/2 x 38 1/2
West Chester University

10. Uplanders at the New Court House
[Unfinished Court House at Turk's Head Threatened by Uplanders Opposed to Relocation of County Seat]
1974
Oil on panel
29 1/2 x 47 1/2
Ann C. Hemphill

11. "Turk's Head" (West Side, High and Market St.)
1974
Pastel
22 1/2 x 38 1/2
Fred T. Cadmus III

12. Sketch for "Turk's Head"
1974
Pencil
4 x 10
Mr. and Mrs. W. Whitman Ball

13. "Turk's Head" (East Side, High and Market St.)
1974
Pastel
18 1/2 x 38 1/2
Fred T. Cadmus III

14. Turk's Head Log Schoolhouse
1975
Oil on panel
13 3/8 x 23 5/8
Dr. and Mrs. Harold H. Wingerd, Jr.

15. Old Horticultural Hall
1976
Pastel
24 1/2 x 37 1/2
Chester County Historical Society

The History Paintings

16. Study for Sentry at Birmingham
1959
Oil on panel
16 1/8 x 19 1/8
Mr. and Mrs. James C. Sorber

17. Sentry at Birmingham
1959
Oil on panel
37 1/2 x 49 1/2
Mr. and Mrs. James C. Sorber

18. Jefferis Ford, Sept. 11, 1777
[Chris Sanderson Musing over Cornwallis' Crossing the Brandywine, 9/11/1777]
1964
Pastel
18 1/2 x 38 1/2
Fred T. Cadmus III

19. The Trap Was Sprung
[General Cornwallis Crossing at Jefferis Ford, Sept. 11,1777]
1968
Oil on panel
29 1/2 x 47 1/2
Lydia Willets Bartholomew

20. Revolutionary Soldier
1970
Oil on panel
11 1/2 x 29 1/2
Lydia Willets Bartholomew

21. Gettysburg, around 3 p.m., July 3, 1863
[The Forming of Pickett's Charge, July 3, 1863]
1971
Oil on gesso board
23 1/2 x 47 1/2
Ann and Alex Giorgiani

22. Squire Cheney "Chester County Patriot"
1972
Oil on gesso board
9 1/4 x 19 1/2
Ann and Alan Clark

23. Sketch for A Chesterbrook Barn
1974
Pencil
12 x 18 1/4
Mr. and Mrs. W. Whitman Ball

24. A Chesterbrook Barn
1974
Oil on gesso board
19 3/8 x 16 1/8
Jean M. Oakes

25. The Revolutionary War Hospital at Yellow Springs
1975
Oil on panel
29 1/4 x 47 1/4
Dr. and Mrs. Henry A. Jordan

Landscapes

26. Brandywine, East Branch
1958
Oil on gesso board
23 1/4 x 47 1/2
Penelope P. Wilson

27. Shaw's Bridge [Northbrook Bridge]
Undated
Pastel
12 3/4 x 30 1/2
William and Elinor Taylor

28. The Corn Field
1960
Pastel
16 5/8 x 38 1/2
Mr. and Mrs. George T. Maher

29. In Full Cry [Fox Hunting Near Lenape]
1963
Pastel
12 3/4 x 38 3/4
Fred T. Cadmus III

30. Andrew Wyeth's Mill
1964
Oil on gesso panel
23 1/2 x 47 1/2
Gerry Lenfest

31. Spring Snow
1965
Pastel
28 x 38 1/2
Gerry Lenfest

32. "After the Rain" [Sykes Farm at Rte 842 and the Brandywine]
1965
Pastel
16 5/8 x 39
Mr. and Mrs. Ralph L. Easter

33. Farmhouse on Winter Night
1965
Pastel
16 1/2 x 38 1/2
Gerry Lenfest

34. 1724 House built by Abiah Taylor
1966
Pastel
28 1/2 x 38 3/4
Gerry Lenfest

35. The Four Seasons
1966
Oil on canvas
35 1/2 x 71 1/2
Commonwealth Bank

36. Deborah's Rock [looking south]
1967
Pastel
22 1/2 x 38 1/2
Fred T. Cadmus III

37. Deborah's Rock [looking north]
1967
Oil on canvas
35 1/2 x 47 1/2
Gerry Lenfest

38. Sleigh Ride [Dilworthtown Oak]
1968
Pastel
18 1/2 x 38 1/4
Mr. and Mrs. Boyd C. Davis

39. Boys Along the Brandywine
1969
Pastel
22 1/4 x 38 1/4
Dr. and Mrs. Earl T. Lewis

40. Early Morning in January
1970
Oil on gesso board
17 3/8 x 47 1/2
Gerry Lenfest

41. Freight Up from Wawaset
1970
Oil on panel
19 3/8 x 47 3/8
Mary G. Warden

42. Bradford Friends Meeting
1970
Oil on gesso board
13 1/2 x 29 3/8
Ethel L. Reagan

43. Moonlight on the Brandywine
1971
Oil on canvas
17 1/2 x 23 1/2
Gerry Lenfest

44. Landscape Sketch [Old Brinton Farm]
1970
Pencil
11 5/8 x 29 5/8
Gerry Lenfest

45. Homestead Near Birmingham
[Thornbury Farm]
1971
Oil on gesso board
15 3/8 x 29 3/8
Thomas and Sandra Spackman

46. Sunrise on the Brandywine Meadow
1971
Oil on gesso board
15 3/8 x 29 3/8
Mr. and Mrs. Nicholas Halladay, Sr.

47. From the Car Window
1971
Oil on gesso board
15 1/2 x 29 1/2
Ann and Alan Clark

48. July Storm [Summer Grain Field with Lightning: Brandywine Valley in Distance]
Undated
Pastel
11 1/4 x 29 1/8
Fred T. Cadmus III

49. Plowing Time
Undated
Pastel
14 1/2 x 38 1/2
Thomas and Sandra Spackman

50. Fireworks – Fourth of July, Looking Out Over Lenape
1972
Oil on panel
11 1/2 x 23 1/4
Gerry Lenfest

51. Pewter Country
1973
Oil on gesso panel
25 3/8 x 47 3/8
Gerry Lenfest

52. The Country Doctor's Visit
1973
Oil on panel
17 5/8 x 47 5/8
Gerry Lenfest

53. Late Afternoon on Brandywine Battlefield
1973
Oil on panel
9 1/4 x 19 1/2
Gerry Lenfest

54. Memories of Our Farm
1975
Oil on panel
17 1/4 x 37 1/4
Mrs. Orville R. March

55. Sconnelltown Hill
1978
Oil on panel
29 1/2 x 47 1/2
Commonwealth Bank

Still Life Paintings

56. Generations
1950
Oil on gesso board
35 1/2 x 47 1/2
Mr. and Mrs. James C. Sorber

57. Iris [Study for Memorial Day]
1950
Charcoal and pastel
21 x 17
Gerry Lenfest

58. Memorial Day
1951
Oil on gesso panel
29 3/4 x 47 3/4
Gerry Lenfest

59. It's Raining
1951
Oil on gesso panel
40 1/4 x 33 1/4
Gerry Lenfest

60. Ripe Tomatoes
[Sketch for Tomatoes on Windowsill]
1952
Pastel
8 x 15 1/2
Gerry Lenfest

61. Sketch for The Open Drawer
1954
Pencil
21 x 17
Mark and Ghisele Curcio

62. The Open Drawer
1954
Oil on gesso panel
40 1/2 x 33 3/8
Gerry Lenfest

63. Lilacs on a Chest
1965
Pastel
23 3/8 x 38 1/4
Edward and Jean E. Cotter

64. "The Fallen Soldier" [Nov. 22, 1963, A Remembrance of the Kennedy Assassination]
1966
Pastel
23 1/2 x 34 3/8
Mr. and Mrs. Ralph L. Easter

65. The Day of the Eclipse
1970
Oil on gesso panel
19 1/2 x 47 3/8
Gerry Lenfest

Portraits

66. Portrait of Wilmer W. MacElree
1950
Oil on masonite
28 3/4 x 40
Chester County Historical Society

67. Portrait of André (Age 2 1/2)
1954
Oil on panel
19 3/8 x 23 3/8
Mrs. Barclay Rubincam

68. Study for The Collector
1955
Pencil
6 3/4 x 5 5/8
Mr. and Mrs. James C. Sorber

69. The Collector (Portrait of James C. Sorber)
1956
Oil on panel
35 1/4 x 29 1/4
Mr. and Mrs. James C. Sorber

70. Portrait of Nelda Jane Davis
1964
Pastel
34 x 28
Mr. and Mrs. Boyd C. Davis